AMERICA

LOVE IT - BUY IT - CHANGE IT

AMERICA

LOVE IT–BUY IT–CHANGE IT

Achieving Wealth and
Social Justice For All

Bruce A. Rowland, LNHA

Banana Split Marketing LLC
4800 Baseline Road E104-246
Boulder, Colorado 80303
www.FinancialBananaSplit.com

Library of Congress Cataloging-in-Publication Data:

Rowland, Bruce A. 1956 -
America : Love It -Buy It - Change It: Achieving Wealth And
Social Justice For All/ Bruce A. Rowland
ISBN Paperback: 978-0-9993704-2-1
ISBN eBook: 978-0-9993704 3-8

Ordering information: Special discounts are available on quantity purchases. For details, contact the publisher.

Cover and Interior Design: Ghislain Viau

Printed in the United States of America

*To everyone who wants to be on the path
of least resistance to happiness and wealth.*

Contents

STEP TWO: ACHIEVE FINANCIAL LITERACY

STEP THREE: COLLABORATE FOR WEALTH BUILDING

STEP FOUR: A PATH TO SOCIAL JUSTICE

INTRODUCTION

Overview

I believe America is at her strongest and Americans are at their best when we're united in a goal for the common good.

Major examples include instituting eighth-grade compulsory education for all children in 1918, defeating fascism in the 1940s by entering World War II, and being the first and only country to land a man on the moon with our space program in 1969.

One obstacle blocking our ability to unify and take action today for the common good is the wide and growing income gap between the haves and the have-nots, illustrated below:

The graphs on the next page from the Congressional Budget Office illustrate that the average income and the national share of income for the highest 1% of income earners (the wealthy) have enjoyed huge gains since 1980. This equals the total returns (growth + dividends) of the general U.S. stock market during this same period. (See: www. FinancialBananaSplit.com for info.) This is a major contributor (fair or not) towards economic inequality and social injustice.

How to level the playing field? Follow the rich: invest in the stock market! But where, when and how to invest? I make it easy: See Ingredient Five: Investing for Wealth and Retirement.

AVERAGE HOUSEHOLD INCOME
before taxes

CHANGE IN SHARE OF INCOME
vs. 1979, after taxes

2007 dollars. Source: Congressional Budget Office

Source: Congressional Budget Office

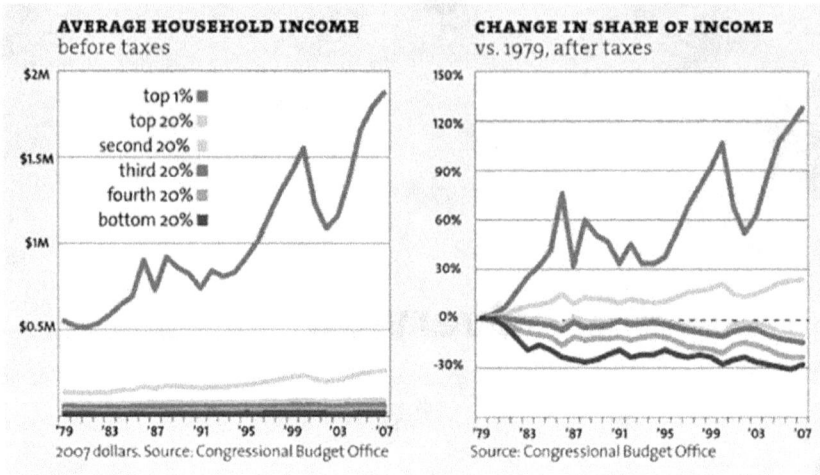

Money is the root cause of social injustice: economic injustice reduces political power which leads to social injustice. That's the bad news. The good news? With this book's information almost anyone can build substantial personal wealth. And work with others to reverse today's economic and political trends to flow from the few back to the many. Goal? To be a nation in spirit and substance "by, for and of the people". (Abraham Lincoln) This book's purpose is to help you and others achieve these goals. How? Self-empowerment using Steps One, Two and Three. Then group empowerment using Step Four to work within our economic and political systems. This, by redirecting the wealth and power of our great country to benefit the vast majority of citizens. This strengthens our country's power and stability long term by strengthening our citizens.

The information is presented as follows:

(Note: All the information contained in Steps One, Two, and Three appear in the book *Building Your Best Financial Banana Split*, courtesy of Banana Split Marketing LLC, 2017).

4

STEP ONE   –   Gain Money Self-awareness:
Money is emotional. We explore your childhood relationship to money and how it affects your present-day financial decisions. You'll use inner-child techniques and haiku poetry to develop a unique Power Money Mantra to gain emotional control over and develop your wealth.

STEP TWO   –   Achieve Financial Literacy:
If you love ice cream and need more money, you'll eat up this financial information. I use a banana split model to simplify and explain financial concepts such as cash flow and investing.

STEP THREE   –   Collaborate for Wealth Building:
With a little help from your friends, I show you how to buy a house using far less money than you imagined. It's all explained in detail, with examples, along with general collaboration techniques enabling you to live life more efficiently.

STEP FOUR   –   A Path to Social Justice:
There are two ways to vote in our country: as a citizen and as a stockholder. A large block of voting stock can influence corporate behavior. We'll explore ways in which the many can speak as one powerful voice to influence change for the common good. Banking and modes of control are also examined.

These four steps and their actions are what is meant by the book's title: *AMERICA: Love It - Buy It - Change It.*

1
Ice Cream Makes Me Happy

At the moment you sink your mouth into a sweet, creamy, scoop of ice cream . . . your eyes close, and your nostrils widen as you deeply inhale the sweetened air below. Your mind drifts into the soft cloud of a happy daydream.

It can be a simple vanilla soft serve enjoyed outside a drive- up window on a hot summer day or a complex scoop of bourbon-infused banana ice cream with dark chocolate ribbons, flecked with pieces of honey-glazed toasted almonds, eaten in front of a roaring fireplace on a dark and stormy night.

These words easily transport us to a positive, comfortable place because the language of ice cream is familiar and understood – not the least bit frightening.

This book's goal is to make your relationship with money positive, comfortable, familiar, and understood – not the least bit frightening.

This will enable you to achieve the American Dream: home ownership and financial security with emotional contentment.

Goal: Rewrite your STORY and . . . unlock your DESTINY.

2

Financial Literature and Food Analogies

I'll use a banana split metaphor to help you easily digest real- world money concepts such as cash flow, credit, and investing.

I chose an ice cream metaphor. It's a happy, relatable pleasure.

Question? Why does the financial industry so often equate money with food? Answer: Food is universally relatable:

- Pure Vanilla Fund = A moderate-risk mutual fund containing a mix of securities (stocks and bonds).
- Cash Cow = Asset that generates a large, steady cash flow.
- Blended Assets = A mix of asset classes in one fund: stocks, bonds, real estate, commodities.
- Churning = Buying and selling securities many times to generate brokerage commissions.
- Market Basket = A variety of assets that closely reflect a given economic market value.
- Spreads = The difference in value between two or more financial measures.

- Turnovers = The amount of times an asset is bought and sold in a given period.
- Yield = The financial return an asset gives its investors.
- Easily Digestible = An easy-to-understand financial term or concept.

When financial terms and concepts relate to something happy and non-threatening, they're easier to digest.

Learning to deal with money can be threatening because it activates fear – our most basic survival instinct. Any threat to our money could be a threat to our survival. We still require food to survive, but now it's acquired using money in a supermarket, not hunting for it in the wild.

Knowledge of money defeats fear of money.

The unknown becomes known. Knowledge becomes your weapon to gather resources successfully to survive in our modern world. So, take your first bite, dig in, and enjoy your "Just desserts" on your path to the American Dream.

3

Banana Split Financial Analogies

My goal is to write a financial book everyone can relate to. Why not base the financial part (step two) directly on food – something familiar and fun – like a banana split? It's about as relatable as something can be.

Step Two: Achieve Financial Literacy uses six ingredients:

1. The Dish = **Cash Flow and Banking.**
2. The Banana = **Home Ownership.**
3. Ice Cream = **Loans, Credit and Debt.**
4. Toppings = **Avoiding Financial Landmines.**
5. Whipped Cream = **Investing for Wealth and Retirement.**
6. Cherry on Top = **Goodwill and Charity.**

They're all detailed in Step Two: Achieve Financial Literacy.

4

Questions and Answers

Who are you financially: Broke student? Non-homeowning millennial? Homeowner unable to retire? Parent wanting to help? Employer/professional seeking to convey advice?

Where do you want to be financially in 10 years? How do you plan to get there? Ask yourself these questions now . . . and again after you've finished the book.

I believe your answers and feelings will change from "I don't know" and "powerless and confused" to "empowered and ready to take control of my financial life" and "ready to make my money work harder for me."

Ready – set – go secure the financial future you deserve!

5

The Whole Self Wealth Program: What, Why, and How?

The Whole Self Wealth Program is a self-improvement program designed to engage and improve your whole Self – emotional, intellectual, physical, spiritual, and financial – to act and interact towards achieving your life's financial goals.

We will be discussing how to apply this program specifically to activate greater financial potential throughout this book.

The **three steps** in the program are:

Step One: Gain Money Self-Awareness: Discover what's broken in your relationship with money and how to fix it. Move more effectively towards your financial goals.

Step Two: Achieve Financial Literacy: Learn what's needed to grow and control wealth to achieve financial goals.

Step Three: Collaborate for Wealth Building: Increase financial leverage by combining resources with others who share the same financial goals.

Each of these steps complements one another, and together, they comprise the Whole Self Wealth Program. The overall goal is to help you achieve the American Dream.

Many books are written either as self-help books or personal financial guides, as if these areas are mutually exclusive . . .

But they're not. We need a balance of wealth and self-wisdom.

I don't view "rich and miserable" or "poor and enlightened," two very different lifestyles, as sustainable or healthy goals. Instead, a combination of self-improvement practices, personal finance techniques, and collaboration strategies enable you to build wealth and attain a clear vision of what really matters. You get the best of both worlds!

Think of the Whole Self Wealth Program as a personal business plan: wealth balanced with self-empowerment. It empowers decision making by helping you understand your relationship to money. This enables you to control money and achieve financial success with emotional contentment. These are all steps on the path to your American Dream.

NOTE: It's not necessary to memorize everything in this book. Read through it once to discover all the information inside then use it as a reference book to review or implement specific subjects, as needed. Also, feel free to look ahead to any subject your curious about. Each heading and subheading is informative in its own right.

6

Author's Personal Story

My family history, education, career, values, and life events give me a unique perspective, interest, and authority to write this book about how to achieve your own American Dream.

I had a deep respect for and warm relationship with my grandfather, Joseph Rowland.

Joseph came to America from eastern Europe in 1908, the oldest son of an immigrant family, and settled in a poor section of Philadelphia. He spoke little English and was taken out of school in the sixth grade and put to work selling newspapers on a street corner for a penny each.

The newspaper sales boss brought my grandfather to the local boxing club, where he learned to protect himself from street toughs who harassed him.

Joseph took to boxing so well his boss became his manager. He turned professional and became a prize fighter. This was his way out of his tenement neighborhood, and several prize fights were soon arranged.

Joseph won them all, collected $500 in prize money, and hung up his boxing gloves to find a business. After he worked as an apprentice in a local butcher shop for several months, he learned enough to set up his own small neighborhood butcher shop. Joseph worked hard, things went well, and soon he was able to save enough money to open a larger shop in Philadelphia not far from where, five years earlier, he had been just another poor kid trying to survive.

His store thrived. He bought a large home and lived "the good life" while raising his family in suburban Philadelphia.

It's this respect for my grandfather, who started from nothing and built himself up through hard work, determination, and overcoming obstacles to achieve the American Dream, that inspired me to fight on and work hard to achieve my own American Dream.

My story is also one of working against obstacles to achieve success: I studied accounting in college and hated it, failing my first accounting test with a 39. My professor suggested I switch majors – liberal arts? I really didn't know what to do, so I figured my parents were right – I should "learn to earn." I continued my studies. I thought of my grandfather's perseverance and made an even bigger effort. Result? I graduated, worked hard, and retired a millionaire at 39.

As a counterbalance to accounting, I also studied philosophy. I took my first philosophy course simply at the suggestion of a friend, asking him which college elective I should take. I took Introduction to Philosophy and was hooked. Philosophers write in the abstract on ethics, science, politics, etc. The student's task is to read and interpret these writings and distill them into an easier-to-understand format. In other words: Creating Order from Chaos.

At age 26, I took over my family's nursing home business. I replaced the previous administrator, who was forced to resign because she couldn't keep up with the demands of the modern era. I had to show constant improvement for the business to survive. I worked 90 hours a week for a year and a half, from dawn till night, seven days a week for 18 months. I remembered my grandfather's work ethic and toughed it out.

All went well, and I turned the nursing home into a success: Creating Order from Chaos. I credit my study of philosophy for keeping me on a principled path during a stormy journey.

Then I started another business, a medical staffing agency. My partner was a savvy Filipino who recruited nurses while I used my good reputation in healthcare to obtain major clients. I was again successful, putting together a business from nothing and turning regulations and business concepts into a working reality: Creating Order from Chaos.

When I was 39, I got an offer I couldn't refuse: Investors wanted to purchase my well-run, profitable nursing home and were willing to pay a big premium. I was ready to leave and start anew.

I hired a financial advisor, invested several million dollars in the market, retired, and saw the world: Great Wall of China, Caribbean sailing, European travels. End of story . . . NOT!

It's true I was financially set and retired at 39, but there was "trouble in paradise."

I wasn't paying attention to my money. It was exposed to great risk while others made gains from it. It wasn't structured to support my financial future. I hadn't thought yet in terms of a Whole Self Wealth Program, as illustrated in this book:

Step One – Gain Money Self-awareness

Step Two – Achieve Financial Literacy

Step Three – Collaborate for Wealth Building

Step One: Gain Money Self-Awareness was missing because I didn't realize I lacked a respectful, positive relationship with money. This would have enabled me to successfully manage it myself. I eventually made the effort to educate my whole Self, including the all-important emotional component of personal finance.

Step Two: Gain Financial Literacy was missing because I hadn't learned personal money management. I couldn't evaluate financial strategies because I didn't understand basic principals.

Step Three: Collaborate for Wealth Building was missing because I trusted certain financial professionals who had much to gain by putting their best interests ahead of mine. They were able to do so because I didn't understand the dynamics of a healthy broker/client relationship – I should have been an active participant.

Should you use a financial advisor? I review the pros and cons in Ingredient Five: Investing for Wealth and Retirement.

After taking a huge financial loss in the 2001 "dot-com" stock market bust, I realized the best person to trust with my money was me – if I was willing to make the effort to educate myself on everything noted above. Good news – I was, I did, and now I'm happy to share it with you!

These financial losses represented more than simply money. They represented years of hard work and sacrifice – 20 years of my life. This loss was also a refection of my own broken relationship with money.

There's an old saying: "You have to be your own doctor." This means you're ultimately responsible for the outcome of your own decisions even if the advice and opinions you considered were given honestly and with good intentions.

This same applies to our finances. No matter what advice and opinions we seek or are given, we need to do our own homework and weigh the consequences of different decisions because, ultimately, no one is responsible for our well-being – physical or financial – except ourselves.

I practice what I teach here: Achieve money self-awareness, gain financial literacy, and collaborate for wealth building. I reorganized my investments to best suit my needs.

Now I have a more-than-enough monthly cash flow as well as participation in the general financial markets.

What took me 61 years to learn can now be learned by you in five hours by reading this one book – congratulations!

The takeaway from all my experience in business and investing can be summed up simply:

You lose what you can't/don't/won't control.

This book helps you control your money and direct your financial destiny. Try it. It's easier than you – or I – thought.

7

True Story – Employee

Can you achieve the American Dream if you start with nothing? Here's a true story illustrating that, with the right mindset, you can !

While I was operating a facility as a licensed nursing home administrator (LNHA) in the Bronx, NY, a longtime employee came to me in tears.

She told me she'd been evicted from her apartment along with her young son and her sister's asthmatic child. She asked if I could somehow help her regain her residence.

Her job was steady, with good pay and benefits, but her boyfriend had "borrowed" several months of rent money, and she had been evicted for non-payment. I called the sheriff's office but was told back-rent charges had to be paid in full before the housing authority would remove the door locks.

Since young children were involved and she was an excellent employee, I offered to loan her money to repay her debt ($3,500) if she agreed to automatic payroll deductions until the loan was paid back. She agreed.

She and the children returned to their apartment, and she got rid of her "boyfriend."

The loan was paid back in full and on time.

Later, I learned she had never stopped the automatic payroll deductions I'd set up as her employer. She and I were ahead of our time with the simple, now widely accepted wealth-growing technique known as automatic deductions – we just didn't know there was a name for it.

After implementing these automatic deductions, she must have made adjustments to her lifestyle (budgeting), because she was also able to fund a savings account. Before I left the business and New York – over 20 years ago – she told me she had saved over $5,000 dollars.

Moral of the Story

If a victimized, urban, single mother of two – broke, in debt, and evicted from a public housing project – can pull herself together, learn to budget, and accumulate thousands in savings . . .

SO CAN YOU!!

STEP ONE

GAIN MONEY
SELF-AWARENESS

1

Understanding And Asserting Your Core Self

Human beings have a great capacity for self-expression. Our ability to express ourselves is our gift, our humanity. It's present in our art, science, engineering, and politics. We tell the world "our story" – who we are – every day, expressing it in our words and deeds (actions).

Are we impulsive, without regard for our future? Or are we deliberate, weighing all potential choices? We're both impulsive and deliberate, and you need to understand and find your own unique balance to successfully gain and control wealth.

Most financial authors give you stories of how Jayne or Jimmie or a member of their family dealt with a financial situation relative to the information provided. Their purpose is to help you navigate similar circumstances. But you're not any of those people. You're a unique individual reacting in a particular way to a particular situation, different from anyone else.

My book prepares you for these encounters, not only by arming you with financial information, but also by helping you understand your Self relative to these financial situations. This enables you to decide which choice is consistent with your goals as an individual – which speaks to your "core values."

Core values make you who you are and guide your life. They represent what matters to you, and they drive how you make decisions and live. Examples include honesty, logic, humor, control, family, fairness, love, religious faith, ambition, intuition, discipline, knowledge, freedom, etc.

We all have these to some degree. It's how we actively prioritize them that makes us unique . . . individuals.

Self-awareness requires examining and understanding what makes you "tick," your personal hierarchy of core values – what's important, what's not.

"Know thyself." (Socrates, ancient Greek philosopher)

Money Self-awareness

Money Self-awareness is understanding your core values, their relationship to money, and adapting them for financial success.

Our brains are "hardwired" to make rapid decisions, shown often in our "fight or flight" reaction which overrides but returns to our core values. It's a mechanism left over from caveman times necessary for our physical survival: Should I stay and fight the saber-toothed tiger or escape up the tree?

Financial decisions are almost never an emergency.
They deserve study – not quick emotional reactions.

Yet our ancestral danger response system is triggered when we're confronted with a financial situation. Why? Because money is key to our modern survival. Any perceived threat to it rattles us. We must regain control. Ancestral, by definition, relates to family.

Our relationship to money is reinforced generation after generation within our own family, where money plays a pivotal role in shaping our core values, including our self-esteem (Orman,1997).

By examining and understanding your family's relationship to money, the influence it had on you as a child, and how it continues to mold your relationship with money today, you can learn and implement techniques for gaining control over financial decisions and, at the same time, realign your core values to serve you better financially. This enables you to triumph over ingrained, potentially limiting family money values.

Self-awareness translated into financial activity equals: emotional control.

This enables us to make thoughtful decisions based on facts and precedent instead of emotional knee-jerk reactions to financial challenges. The results: better decisions and greater returns (profits) with less emotional, and thus financial, volatility.

Our ability to influence "macro" (large) economic events is minimal: the national economy, the stock market, a company's annual earnings, etc. Our ability to influence our own behavior when experiencing these events is huge and critical for personal financial success.

The world's greatest thinkers and achievers have similar thoughts on the importance of emotional control:

- "What we think, we become."   (Buddha)
- "The inevitable must be accepted and turned to advantage."   (Napoleon)
- "Life belongs to the living. And he who lives must be prepared for changes."   (Goethe)
- "A person who never made a mistake, never tried anything new."   (Einstein)

- "Genius is the ability to renew one's emotions
  in daily experience." (Cezanne)

Goal: Rewrite your STORY and . . . unlock your DESTINY.

My point: Whether you're a hippie or hedge fund manager, you need to understand your Self, thereby understanding how money affects you emotionally, to deal with money successfully. This fact comes into play even more, and its importance is multiplied, when you engage with others in collaboration, especially multi-year collaboration such as becoming a shareholder in home ownership (detailed in Step Three).

To advance ourselves financially, we need to understand our past and current relationships with money and then forge a new, realistic money relationship based on our unique core values and goals.

The following techniques will help you clarify your core values and goals. This enables you to better assert yourself, streamlining your efforts on your path to financial success.

2

Understanding Your Self
& Techniques

Read All About It

The book The ABC'S of Self by Dawn Bogar provides a simple yet effective way to understand and connect with your Self's core values. Its brief messages and exercises are an easy way to jumpstart self-refection and recognize a relationship with your Self:

> You can become aware of your Self right now. Be seated for a minute and just pay attention. How does your body feel? Are your muscles tense, or are they relaxed? Does your breathing seem fast, slow, or regular? What were you thinking a minute ago? When you look in the mirror, what are the eyes saying?
>
> —Bogar, 2013

Link to this book: www.FinancialBananaSplit.com

Money Feelings – A Self Examination

What thoughts about money currently make you fearful? Write them down in a word(s) or phrase(s) for later use.

Examples could include paying next month's rent or mortgage, mounting credit card debt, paying for school, etc. (Orman, 1997).

It's an important link to your current attitude towards money. You'll use these in a brief writing exercise, where you'll develop your own unique "Power Money Mantra." (A mantra is a repeated phrase that expresses a strong belief).

Your Hidden Money Memories

Think of your oldest sweater or jeans hanging in the back of your closet or buried deep in your dresser drawer. You've forgotten about them. They don't fit. They're not useful.

This describes most people's current attitudes towards money: It was acquired years ago. You still own it. It no longer fits. It's not useful to you anymore. It needs updating.

Most of us form our understanding and relationship to money when we're children, taking our cue from our family (Orman, 1997).

Take a moment to think about your family's money dynamics. Especially try to remember one specific incident, good or bad, that triggered your sense of money's worth and your relationship to it (Orman, 1997).

Write it down in a word(s) or phrase for use later in the book. Examples could include fear, joy, always/never enough, etc. It's an important link to your past that you'll use in a brief writing exercise where you'll develop your own Power Money Mantra.

True Story – Thermostat

I recall an incident in my own childhood when I first became aware of the importance of money, my relationship to it, and the effect it could have on my life. I assumed money wasn't an issue, as I never wanted for anything. The weekend weather for the neighborhood football game was my biggest concern.

One day, during winter, I felt cold, so I turned up the heating thermostat in our house. I just turned it clockwise, far to the right, probably up to eighty degrees.

A few moments later, my father yelled out, "Who turned the heat so far up?" I said, "I did because I was cold." My mother shouted, "If you're cold, go put on a sweater and don't touch the heat again . . . It's too expensive."

I was shocked. I couldn't believe my family actually had to worry about the cost of a basic comfort like heating our home. At that very moment, I understood for the first time in my life the importance of money and the affect it could have on me. This served me well later in my business career when I was in the position to sink or swim. I chose to swim and metaphorically stay warm.

Your Inner Child Is Waiting to Meet You

The idea of an "inner child" was originally proposed by psychiatrist Carl Jung in the 19th century. He referred to this phenomenon as the "puella complex" (wikipedia.org). This concept was popularized in 1968 by Dr. Eric Berne in his book Transactional Analysis.

He suggested that at any one time, we act in either our child, adult, or parent mode, switching between them to deal more effectively with day-to-day life circumstances:

Child mode = Emotional and impulsive

Adult mode = Reasonable and purposeful

Parent mode = Stern and controlling

I chose the child mode because, as children, we receive family money messages and continue to harbor these into adulthood (Orman, 1997). It's the child we need to redirect in order for our adult attitudes to change, because children act on instinct. Adults use reason.

Understand your inner child, and you'll understand yourself, thus opening the door for change and growth, including financial growth by injecting reason into financial decisons.

When you access your inner child and ask him/her with words or thoughts if something is right or wrong for you . . . you'll feel their response immediately. I did.

You can meet and interact with your inner child by doing the following exercises (Capacchione, 1991):

Drawing Exercise

Our dominant hand is the hand we're trained to write with. It's been taught to practice patience and control, like an adult. Our non-dominant hand is untrained and childlike.

- Obtain blank, unlined paper and a writing implement.
- Sit somewhere quiet and relaxing where you can concentrate.
- Imagine a beautiful, safe place where you can meet with your inner child as if you want to be alone to pray.
- Close your eyes and imagine both of you are there.
- Now open your eyes and, with your non-dominant hand, let your inner child draw a picture of himself or herself.

What does the child in the picture seem to be saying to you? Ask him or her about a childhood money memory. What is their response? How do you respond? Does something need to be addressed or changed for the future concerning this?

Reflect upon your experience to become more in tune with your inner child. Was this a pleasant or stressful experience? Did it flow, or were you critical?

This indicates your current relationship status with your inner child. This changes over time, as all relationships do. Reflect upon and repeat this exercise periodically to discover what changes might be occurring.

Let's Talk

Another exercise to help you interact with your inner child is a simple conversation. Use your dominant hand to write a question. Use your other hand to let your inner child answer. You'll notice your inner child's handwriting is similar to a five-year-old's and that he or she might answer in a simple but direct manner.

Sample Conversation

Adult: Hello, child. I would be happy to meet you.

Child: Me too!! You're nice!!

Adult: What is your name?

Child: My name is -----------------.

Adult: What would you like to do now?

Child: Talk and laugh together!!

Since you've now established a relationship with your inner child, review your Recall Your Past and Confront Your Fears questions and answers and modify as appropriate, based on your interaction with your inner child.

Does your inner child help you remember the past and give you a clearer or deeper understanding of your family's financial messages? This will help you write a more meaningful Power Money Mantra, which will help you advance financial goals, moving you towards the American Dream.

Want Power? Unleash Your Creativity!

Our survival instincts reside in the primitive part of our brain (cerebellum), and our intellect and creativity reside in the modern part of our brain (cerebrum/cerebral cortex). This exercise uses your intelligence (modern part) to override your emotions (primitive part) to power through financial obstacles.

The goal is to create a unique Power Money Mantra related to the vision you want for your future in view of the personal history you need to override. We'll use a short-verse, three-line format similar to but simpler than Japanese haiku (traditional three-line structured poetry). This promotes meaningful, focused thinking, easy to remember.

To start, here are samples of my own haiku/short verse:

I

Winter: Geese fly noisily overhead
Plants: buried – silent – patience
They wait to burst forth: Spring

II

Thoughts swirl like confetti in my brain
Not New Year's. No big-city parade.
As I approach the bar . . . our eyes connect

III

Summer, autumn, winter, spring
Summer, autumn, winter, spring
A good joke transcends the seasons

Note your reaction: contemplative, curiosity, amused? Haiku/ short verse provoke thoughts and feelings yet are simple and focused.

Next we'll use basic guidelines to write short verse: The first one is general, and the next one is financial – this will be your unique Power Money Mantra.

These short verse will be three lines each. Each line will contain at least one of the references below:

One line contains the subject – the main focus of your writing.

One line contains living /nature – it's universally relatable.

One line contains action – giving your writing depth and interest.

The lines can be in any order. One line may contain multiple references as long as all three reference types are used in your work.

Use words or phrases from the Read All about It, Money Feelings, Your Hidden Money Memory, and Inner Child exercises, as appropriate.

Use my examples to help you create yours. Now it's time to write our general-subject short verse:

ME

Standing on the front porch   (action, natural world)
... loud sniffing behind door   (action, natural world)
family dog, anxious to greet me   (subject, action, action)

YOU

Now let's write our Power Money Mantras:

ME

Family says: Money solves all problems
Reality says: Hard shell equals poverty within
Truth says: People first – richness will follow

YOU

This is your **Power Money Mantra** and your new story. Repeat it often to keep your financial goals on track.

Share your unique Power Money Mantra in a written, video or recorded music format(s) with us at: www.FinancialBananaSplit.com.

3

Asserting Yourself & Techniques

Asserting means communicating your preferences to others in order to protect or advance your interests, including financial interests. You assert your right to say no when someone insists you take an action that's inconsistent with your core values, or yes when you want to achieve something aligned with them.

An example could be a salesman trying to convince you to buy an upgrade that would be nice but whose added cost would be a detour on your path to the American Dream.

Asserting requires skills enabling you to understand what is actually being said, to "read between the lines" in order to identify the meaning and intent of the speaker.

To best assert your interests, you first need a clear vision – in detail – of what your goals are and then techniques for achieving them as follows:

Definitions – Visualization and Self-Actualization

Imagining the life you want in detail is Visualization. Achieving the life you want is Self-Actualization.

Albert Einstein, one of our most brilliant scientists, said: "Imagination is more important than knowledge."

True Story – Soldier

Here's a true story of a soldier turning visualization into self- actualization.

During the Vietnam War (1955–75), an American prisoner of war (POW) was held captive in the jungles of Vietnam in a Vietcong prison camp. He endured harsh, primitive conditions including a near- starvation diet and captivity in a bamboo cage, mostly in solitary confinement.

To maintain his sanity during these long, desperate hours, he visualized – over and over – in minute detail everything he could about a day playing golf: the drive from his home to the golf course, the weather, how the grass smelled, the clothes he would be wearing, his golf stance, finger grip, etc.

When the war ended, he was released and returned home. He resumed golfing. Before the war, his average score was in the low 90s. When he played again, he shot a 79, a low score he'd never before achieved (lower scores are better). He continued to play with more accuracy and lower scores.

Using visualization, he imagined in detail playing a better golf game while captive. This technique helped him to not only reach his psychological survival goal but was so powerful it changed him physically by manipulating his muscle memory and helped him self-actualize a better golf game.

www.FinancialBananaSplit.com for a link to the story's website.

Visualization Techniques

- Power Visualization: My term for visualizing goals during cardio exercises like running/swimming/dancing, etc. What's your goal? Visualize it while exercising.

- Relaxed Visualization: My term for visualizing goals during passive exercise like meditation, yoga, etc. Contemplate during quiet moments and visualize your desired life's goals in detail: people, places, and objects.

- Arts and Crafts Visualization: My term for visualizing goals by assembling a storyboard of cutout pictures and words to put onto a surface (refrigerator, wall, etc.).

As a writer, I spend many hours working alone researching, writing, and rewriting. I cut out and tape quotes and pictures that inspire, humor, or prompt me to think about life onto a blank page and then tape it onto my office wall. This helps me see the big picture, keep my goals in sight, and continue to work and hope my contributions have value.

These are some of my favorites:

- "You must be the change you want."   (Ghandi)
- "If you're going through Hell, keep going ."   (Churchill)
- "Disaster brings change and opportunity."   (Chinese)
- "You can't depend on your eyes when your imagination is out of focus."   (Twain)

- "A person must pay dearly for the divine
  gift of creative fire."   (Hemingway)
- "Repeal all past history. You still cannot
  repeal human nature."   (Lincoln)
- "We cannot solve problems with the same
  thinking we use to create them."   (Einstein)
- "Life is like riding a bicycle. To keep your
  balance, you must keep moving."   (Einstein)
- "The secret to getting ahead in life is
  getting started."   (Twain)
- "The human race has one really effective
  weapon, and that is laughter."   (Twain)
- "One does not become enlightened
  by imagining figures of light, but by
  making the darkness concious."   (C. Jung)
- "When in doubt, tell the truth."   (Twain)

4

Self-Actualization & Techniques

If the purpose of visualization is to awaken the untapped energy of your imagination, then the purpose of self- actualization is to redirect this energy outward, to influence the world around you to assist in the manifestation of your goals. This is accomplished through communication.

Want to achieve the American Dream? Then learn to communicate effectively. Better communicators express themselves more efficiently. This wastes less of your precious time by helping you avoid unnecessary detours on your path to the American Dream. After all, time is money . . . when you know how to make it. Enhanced communication skills allow you to understand and respond to our world, empowering you to achieve your goals – to actualize them (McKay 2009).

These are:

- Listening skills
- Expression
- Body language

Listening Skills

Listening is an essential skill for making and maintaining relationships to help influence the world around you. It helps us understand and interpret others and lets us see how others understand and interpret us. Good listening skills consist of three actions:

Paraphrasing

Paraphrasing means repeating in your own words the issue(s) the speaker stated. Doing this helps you remember and understand what is said and enables you to process important information.

In addition, paraphrasing compliments the speaker, which let's them know you're listening and consider them important (whatever your opinion).

Repeating what you believe you're hearing in your own words stops miscommunication and false assumptions and cools down heated debate.

A paraphrasing example could begin with "What I hear you saying is ---------" or "Do you mean ----------------------------?"

Clarifying

Clarifying means asking questions to help understand the speaker's thoughts and feelings, to get a clearer picture of what they actually want you to understand.

Asking for more information shows interest and helps the speaker dig deeper into meaningful details, enabling a more informed, impactful response from you.

Clarifying examples might be "What were the circumstances?" or "Did John know you were already working on this issue with Cathy?"

Feedback

Giving feedback is responding by sharing thoughts and feelings.

It deepens your understanding of what the speaker said. Your feedback carries greater weight when it's done in a non- judgmental manner. You become a participant in the communication experience.

A feedback example might be: "Listening to what you said, I really feel . . ."

Expression

You can communicate effectively if you understand and use techniques to express yourself and recognize when others use them. This helps influence the world around you.

Observation

Observation is simply and accurately reporting what you saw, heard, or felt.

Feelings

By sharing your feelings and listening to others' feelings (empathizing), you enhance communication depth. Your goal is to establish a stronger emotional connection. Get "personal" with people, and you win them over. Example: "How's your family?" "What is your dog's name?"

Needs

A need is something necessary that enables you to achieve a specific goal. It's also important for accurate communication. Your needs are tough for someone else to know, and you're the only one who knows exactly what your needs are.

Communicating needs helps to clarify a situation. Example: "I need to be home by 4 pm for my appointment."

Wants

A want is a wish or desire for something that will help you achieve your goal but is not necessary to achieve it.

Wants help others understand the level of importance you place on something. Example: "I want to stop at the supermarket to get milk if you have time."

Assertiveness

Assertiveness is the right to express your thoughts, feelings, wants, and needs. You have the right to: make mistakes, share your opinion, change your mind, protest criticism, negotiate, and say no. You also have the right not to justify your actions. However, be aware when assertiveness turns into aggression. Aggression is part of asserting yourself and usually occurs when danger is present. Aggression ends effective communication because you disregard the other person's needs and seek to end the situation immediately.

Negotiation

Negotiation is the skill that helps you get what you want while still keeping the lines of communication open.

There are four stages to a negotiation:

1. Preparation: Gather all information. Know what you want, what you are willing to give, and the least you'll settle for. Know your options.
2. Discussion: Each side offers their point of view with evidence (or not) and describes why they feel that way.

3. Proposal/Counter proposal: Each side offers proposals and counter proposals in an effort to move closer to an agreement.

4. Agreement/Disagreement: Agreement ends the negotiation. Disagreement brings it back to stage #2 or #3 until an agreement is reached or negotiations end with no agreement.

Example: Pat: "I feel I should have the master bedroom because its bathroom has the only bathtub in the house. I spend hours at a time bathing with my antique toy duck collection, and this would make the downstairs bathroom and its shower more readily available to you and the other house members."

Jane: "How about, instead, you take a regular bedroom and the only garage space exclusively so you don't have to clean snow off your car? Also, this way, you'll always have a parking spot and won't have to look for one on the street."

Pat: "OK. It's a deal. I don't know how much snow we'll get here in Miami, but I like the idea of having a permanent parking garage space."

Body Language

It's understood our body language can have a much greater impact than word choice. Body language includes facial expressions, body movement, and proximity (distance). Use and recognize these to influence the world around you.

Groups of body language signals are the truest indicators:

- Head down, shoulders drooping, arms at sides, feet flat = sad.
- Eyes wide open, animated and standing on the balls of the feet = excited.
- Crossed arms, firm stance, narrowed eyes = anger.

Our ability to recognize these physical signals gives us better opportunities to understand others and modify our own signals.

Conclusion

Learning to communicate effectively is important to successfully engage others in order to determine if someone's proposal is truly in your best interest, financial or otherwise, and to advocate for your preferences. It helps avoid unnecessary and costly detours on the path to your American Dream.

I would've had a better chance of figuring out I was getting a bad deal from previous financial encounters if I'd possessed better communication skills. I could have used clarification/feedback/para-phrasing/ listening/body language/assertiveness to better understand if those financial proposals were in my best interests or not. Now, hopefully, I know better.

Better communicators are happier people.

5

Step One - Conclusion

Money Self-awareness is for understanding, relative to money, who you are, what you want, and how to get there.

If you don't understand your Self . . . how can others?

ACHIEVE
FINANCIAL LITERACY

(Understanding money using six banana split ingredients)

1

Overview

1. **Ingredient One – The Dish: Cash Flow and Banking**
   The foundation: solid, no leaks.
2. **Ingredient Two – The Banana: Home Ownership**
   The defining structure of the Banana Split and the American Dream.
3. **Ingredient Three – Ice Cream: Loans/Credit/Debt**
   Ways to use money are as numerous as ice cream flavors.
4. **Ingredient Four – Toppings: Avoiding Financial Landmines**
   They cover other ingredients and affect their overall flavor.
5. **Ingredient Five – Whipped Cream: Investing for Wealth and Retirement**
   Rapid growth showcases your determination to follow financial plans and quickens your pace towards the American Dream.
6. **Ingredient Six – Cherry On Top: Goodwill and Charity**
   It's concentrated sweetness, giving you purpose and helping direct resources so you feel good about your wealth.

   Together, these ingredients illustrate how to deal successfully with money during the life cycle: saving and spending through retirement.

2

Ingredient One:
Cash Flow And Banking

Cash Flow and Banking are the dish in the banana split. It's the part of your financial plan that has to be solid, no leaks.

> *Being aware of and actively managing your cash flow is the difference between controlling your money or your money controlling you . . . period.*

How much you spend on credit cards, entertainment, food, clothes, or telephone and how much you're able to save need to be informed choices because they tie in directly to your cash flow.

Credit and debt are so impactful to your financial health that they're covered separately in Ingredient Three: Loans, Credit, and Debt.

A budget helps you make informed choices because you'll realize how much available cash you have to spend each month before overspending into debt – explained in detail in the next few pages.

A friend recently asked me: "How does someone blow through a million dollars without realizing it and end up broke?" My answer:

"They didn't pay attention and didn't know or didn't care about cash flow: how much was coming in versus how much was going out."

This scenario famously happens to celebrities all the time.

My Point: If a millionaire superstar can get into financial trouble, **you** must be **aware** of your **cash inflow and outflow**, which is exactly what a budget helps you see.

What causes you to spend beyond your means? Advertising. There's nothing wrong with you. You're human. Advertisers know this and use it to sell you products and services prioritizing their greed over your need.

We fall victim to advertising with strong psychological appeal. Advertisers use behavioral science (the study of behavior) and data gathered from our smart phones, credit card transactions, etc. to understand our buying habits.

They know us better than we know ourselves. Previously, in this book's Step One: Gain Money Self- awareness, you learned techniques to understand and redirect yourself from taking actions that lead to bad money decisions.

You can also resist these ever-present, sophisticated techniques that don't add lasting quality to your life and move you further away from the American Dream with the following techniques:

Cash Flow Defense –
Four Helpful Techniques

(All techniques are explained in detail later in the book)

1) Use the Self-awareness and Communication Techniques in this book's Step One for control and become an informed Consumer. Determine which of your core values the product or service appeals

to, the techniques being used, if you really need it, and, if so, which need (as opposed to want) it fulfills. (Full text version)

After going through this sequence a few times, it becomes automatic. You'll apply it to all future purchase decisions.

2) Start saving for your future now, whether to buy a home or to increase retirement savings, to counter overspending A simple way to accomplish this is by implementing automatic deductions from your paycheck or checking account and transferring these funds into savings. This is using the "out of sight, out of mind" technique (detailed later in the book).

Automatic deductions are a major stepping stone on your path to financial security. This is so important it's detailed again separately in Ingredient Five: Investing.

3) Be a "Conscious Consumer." Earning money takes your time and effort. Have respect for yourself and consider your spending choices in view of this.

You have a lot more control over what you spend . . . than over what you earn.

Before you open your wallet and hand over your money, ask:

- Will I really use this product or service? Is it worth it?
- Can I live without it? How does this change my life?
- Do I own anything else that provides the same use?
- Did I feel a need for this item before I saw it in the store?
- Can I get the same product or service for less elsewhere?

4) Be aware of and track your cash flow using a budget. A sample one-page blank budget is provided on page 59. It's simply adding up all your expenses and then adding up all your income and subtracting one from the other. The net result shows if you spend all, more, or less money every month than you take in – the basic cash flow concept.

Elsewhere in this book are techniques to improve your monthly cash flow by helping you save and grow your wealth.

You can also go to: www.FinancialBananaSplit.com to download apps for services that help you develop a budget and track and manage your money.

These apps allow users to keep track of activity from banks, credit cards, investments, loans, and financial transactions through a single user interface. Users can also create budgets and financial goals.

Feel free to use my format to input your own information. You're looking for realistic numbers – a good guess – not perfection. Your accuracy improves as you complete each monthly budget.

Obtain information from your bank and credit card statements, receipts, checkbook, cash on hand, memory, etc. Looking back on how you spent your money every month will amaze you. It's a real eye opener into your spending habits.

Also, make a list of once-a-year expenses (birthdays, holidays, etc.), add them all together, and divide by twelve. Put this amount in the "Annual Expenses" item of your budget. If you don't spend this amount monthly, you'll have it to spend at the time of year it was meant for: holidays, birthdays, vacations, etc.

YOUR MONTHLY BUDGET

BUDGET EXPENSES	COLUMN 1	COLUMN 2	
Rent or Mtg + Prop. tax	$ ___	Insurance	$ ___
Utilities	$ ___	Clothes/shoes	$ ___
TV/internet	$ ___	Education	$ ___
Phone	$ ___	Student loan expense	$ ___
Car expenses:		Loans: other	$ ___
gas/ins/pkg/maint.	$ ___	Dry-cleaning	$ ___
Salon: hair care/nails, etc.	$ ___	Cosmetics/skin care	$ ___
Pharmacy	$ ___	Health insurance	$ ___
Entertainment	$ ___	Hobbies/sports	$ ___
Travel/vacations	$ ___	Childcare/sitter	$ ___
Food: groceries/delivery, etc.	$ ___	Pet care	$ ___
Kids' allowance/other expenses	$ ___	Charity	$ ___
Subscriptions & club dues	$ ___	Child support	$ ___
Down-payment: future house	$ ___	Alimony	$ ___
Emergency fund: future		Credit card minimum	$ ___
house	$ ___	Other	$ ___
Pension/Investments	$ ___		
Annual expenses	$ ___		
COLUMN 1 TOTAL	$ ___	COLUMN 2 TOTAL	$ ___

Expenses: Column 1 + Column 2 =

TOTAL BUDGET EXPENSES: $ _____

BUDGET INCOME	COLUMN 1	COLUMN 2	
Net salary(s)/wages	$ ___	Child support	$ ___
Bonus/other	$ ___	Alimony	$ ___
Cash income (tips, etc.)	$ ___	Net investment	$ ___
Net refunds (tax, etc.)	$ ___	Income	$ ___
Net rental income	$ ___	Odd jobs/hobby	$ ___
Net other	$ ___	Other	$ ___
		Other	$ ___
COLUMN 1 TOTAL	$ ___	COLUMN 2 TOTAL	$ ___

Income: Column 1 + Column 2 =
TOTAL BUDGET INCOME: $ _____

TOTAL BUDGET INCOME minus
TOTAL BUDGET EXPENSE =

YOUR MONTHLY BUDGET NET AMOUNT (+/-): $ _____

Whatever your monthly budget net amount is, you can increase your surplus or decrease your deficit (so it becomes a surplus) by conducting a basic review of your expenses. Decide which are needs (necessities) and which are wants (desires). Be smart – trade several wants for savings. (Techniques for this are detailed earlier, in Step One: Gain Money Self-awareness. (Full text version)

The most powerful way to cut costs is to plan purchases.

Monthly Budget Transfers

Surplus money can go into your savings account for future home down payment or early mortgage payoff on your existing home, or it can be put into your pension and/or investments.

The easiest way to do this is to implement automatic deductions from your checking account monthly or from every paycheck.

Example: If your take-home pay is $800 dollars every two weeks, have your employer deduct $112 ($8 per day x 14 days) and automatically deposit it into your savings account. Or instruct your bank to transfer twice this amount monthly from your checking account into your savings account.

It's "out of sight, out of mind," and there are no weekly/monthly decisions to be made about whether or not, or how much, to deduct. It keeps these monies out of easy "spending cash" reach. You'll adjust your lifestyle to accommodate to this automatically. (Automatic deductions are detailed later, in Ingredient Five: Investing).

An alternative to a bank is a program offered by the Social Security Administration, part of the federal government. Their free program invests your money in United States Treasury bonds, considered one of the world's safest investments. You can withdraw your money at any time – penalty free. Downside? Slow growth at low interest rates. www.FinancialBananaSplit.com for link to website.

Divorce – Special Note: Money issues are the biggest single cause of divorce. It's a huge roadblock to the American Dream. **Develop a sample monthly budget **now** with your potential mate that you can both agree upon – **before** getting **married.** Work out money issues now before they cause problems.

Banks – A Big Part of Your Cash Flow Picture

Definition: A bank is a financial institution licensed and regulated by the government as a Receiver of Deposited Monies. Banks operate as commercial banks or credit unions. Corporate shareholders own commercial banks. Depositors – as members – own their credit union.

Credit unions generally have lower fees for banking services and are more tied to the local economy with loan programs.

Commercial banks generally have greater ATM access nationally, translating into lower ATM fees out of state.

Deposit insurance: Your money – up to $250,000 per qualified account – is insured against losses arising from a bank failure.

Commercial banks use the Federal Deposit Insurance Corporation (FDIC), and credit unions use the National Credit Union Association (NCUA). They are equally safe programs.

Verify that your bank participates in one of these (there is usually a sign on the door) by asking for proof of membership.

Choosing a Financial Institution

Services include checking and savings accounts, CDs, loans, mortgages, pensions, credit and debit cards, and financial brokers.

Access to banks and credit unions can be made by visiting a physical location (branch), ATM machine, or online by computer or by using your smartphone.

Use the following criteria to choose the right bank for you:

- Convenience: Do you want or need to interact in person? Then choose a bank with a physical location near you.

- Ease of Transactions: How will you conduct your business? In person? Online? Using an app to make deposits by smartphone? Using nearby ATMs? Choose a bank that best fits your lifestyle.

- Interest Rates: Who pays the highest interest rates on the type of accounts you plan to have (savings/CDs, etc.)?

- Fees: What fees are charged for what? When? Credit card? Checking accounts? How many free checks can you write a month? Is there a minimum balance required to avoid a monthly fee?

Two Monthly Financial Tracking "Must Do's"

Whichever financial institution you choose and however you choose to bank, there are two tasks you need to do every month to track your cash flow:

1) REVIEW your monthly bank statement for accuracy: Are all deposits accounted for? Are there any unexplained charges? Does the ending balance of last month's statement match the beginning balance for this month? Any suspicious activity or errors? Your name and address current?

2) BALANCE your monthly bank statement: Instructions are provided on the bank statement or available at the bank or online. This allows you to verify the proper cash flow in your account has occurred.

True Story – A Million-dollar Bank Error

I briefly became a millionaire when I was twelve years old due to a banking clerical error. Here's my story:

When I was growing up in the suburbs in the 1960s, most people banked with their local bank. Adults had checking, savings, and Christmas accounts, and children put part of their birthday or holiday money in little passbook savings accounts. A passbook looked like a passport. Each time you made a deposit or withdrawal, the amount was posted into your passbook on a typewriter by a bank teller. One day, I made a small deposit into my passbook savings account and then went home and put the passbook away in my bedroom dresser drawer and promptly forgot about it.

The next day, the telephone rang – most people had only one telephone in their house, generally hanging on the kitchen wall. Our phone was the standard olive green, rotary dial. My mother answered. She became highly excited from whatever the person on the other end of the line was saying.

She asked me, "Bruce, did you make a deposit with your passbook at the bank yesterday?"

Being a boy, I assumed I must have done something wrong. I replied, "Yes," and my mother said, "Go get it and bring it down here right away!"

So I got the passbook and gave it to my mother. She opened it and exclaimed, "Oh my goodness . . . you're right!" She quickly hung up the phone and showed me my little savings passbook. Instead of posting the total as $100 dollars, the bank teller had put the total as $1,000,000!

I was rich!! . . . for about 24 hours.

My mother instructed me to go to the bank right away, where the embarrassed bank teller corrected her error. She put lines across my newfound million dollars and replaced it with the proper $100.27.

Moral of the Story

Check every detail of your bank and credit card statements every month. You never know when fate will hand you an extra million dollars.

Ingredient One - Conclusion

Cash Flow and Banking are interconnected and is the most important Ingredient to understand and regularly monitor for your financial health.

3

Ingredient Two: Home Ownership

Home Ownership is the banana in the banana split. It defines the banana split and the American Dream.

"The strength of a nation derives from the integrity of the home."
(Confucius, philosopher, 551 B.C.)

Purpose of This Book

The purpose of this book, as I've mentioned, is to enable you to achieve the American Dream, which includes home ownership.

Goal: Rewrite your STORY . . . and unlock your DESTINY.

Your Story

Your story (or that of your child/grandchild) may include one or more of these truths:

- You can't afford a home with your current job.
- You're burdened with student debt.
- You'll never have the financial flexibility to retire.

Home ownership is the key to rewriting your story and unlocking your destiny, because real estate historically rises in value, which gives you:

- A wealth increase that doesn't require another job.
- An asset you can borrow from to pay off student debt.
- An additional income stream – renting all or part of it.

A statistic from the United States Census Bureau reveals the average new home cost $82,500 in 1981 and $242,300 in 2011 – an increase of $159,800 and a 300% gain. This period reflects the term of a standard 30-year mortgage.

My parents bought our family home in 1958 for $36,000. It was a medium-sized split-level design – standard suburbia. It sold in 1998 for $405,000 – a $369,000 increase and a gain of almost 1200% in 40 years.

These examples illustrate long-term home ownership. Sometimes shorter periods have proven disastrous for homeowners, such as the recent mortgage meltdown of 2008. In this case, a house price decline of 75% from its high was not unusual. People lost everything. But it was a great time to buy a home if you could afford it, as my friend June did in True Story – June Cleaver on page 123. I discuss timing considerations for house buying a little later.

Catch up/Step up

Problem: You can't afford to buy a home because you can't save enough money to catch up to ever-increasing down payment requirements due to student loans, etc.

Taking action by implementing this book's three practical steps now makes it possible to become a homeowner with much less cash and income than you thought possible. This puts increasing home values in your favor.

Home Ownership – Quick Overview

A primary purpose of this book is to for you to become a home-owner able to pay off your mortgage sooner than later.

A mortgage is the type of loan used when buying a home.

"Home" refers to the real estate you own and reside in regardless of type: house, condominium, co-op, townhouse, etc.

Home ownership lets you progress from having dreams to making plans, because it stops you from being victimized by ever-increasing rents.

A fixed-rate mortgage on your home (the interest rate never changes) can even decrease if you refinance when interest rates decline (detailed later in this ingredient).

After you pay off your mortgage, your housing costs decline dramatically because you no longer have monthly mortgage payments. Owning becomes much cheaper than renting.

Owning your own home mortgage free is primary financial security because it makes cash flow available to invest towards wealth accumulation (detailed in Ingredient Five: Investing).

On the path towards owning your own home, you'll be able to accomplish other important financial goals too:

1. Increase Your Wealth – Home values historically increase over time. Your home ownership percentage also increases as you pay off your mortgage principal every month.

2. Save for Retirement – Cash saved by not paying rent and put to work in pensions and other investments can grow by themselves (see Ingredient Five: Investing).

3. Pay off Student Loans – Your house is an asset that can be used as collateral to secure a home equity loan at a lower interest rate than your student loan. Calculations for assessing your best loan options are described later in this Ingredient.

Home Ownership –
Your Basic Financial Pathway

Your basic financial pathway to home ownership uses a "step up" approach (detailed on page 158):

Save to become part-owner and then buy your own home:

• Save enough money to purchase a "share" in a collaboratively owned house. You become a shareholder (like a corporate stockholder) while living in this house with others.

• Sell your share later for a profit. Use this as down-payment money to buy your own home. The profit is tax free if used this way – the IRS considers it a "residential rollover."

Example

This is an example of how to follow Home Ownership – Your Basic Financial Pathway:

Example based on house purchase price of $200,000/down payment 10% ($20,000)/your ownership percentage 25% (¼).

1. $8 a day x 365 days = $2,920 (amount saved in one year).
2. $2,920 x 3 years = $8,760 (amount saved in three years).
3. Amounts needed for your 1/4 house ownership:

   $5,000 – Mortgage down-payment.

   $2,275 – House emergency Fund (explained later).

$1,485 – House closing costs (explained later).

$8,760 – Total amount needed = Total amount saved.

4. The house value rises $100,000 in five years from $200,000 to $300,000. Your share = $32,275: $7,275 (Refunded down-payment + house Emergency Fund) plus $25,000 (Your share, 25%, of the $100,000 increase in the house's value).

5. You sell your house share to a new shareholder for $32,275.

6. You use this money to buy a home of your own.

A Word about Crowdfunding

"Crowdfunding," or collaborative funding, has become popular recently and is used by individuals and companies to raise money for projects, especially start-ups, when capital isn't available through traditional channels (banks, etc.). If you're planning on obtaining a mortgage, a traditional lender won't issue you one if you've borrowed money for your down payment. Crowdfunding will not help you obtain a traditional mortgage.

It's possible crowdfunding could be a source for the down payment if the right deal is offered. The crowdfunding participants might insist on a share of the profit when you sell your house share. This defeats the purpose of the "step up" process for home buying and should be kept in mind when evaluating any offer. Also note interest rate and structure offered: fixed/variable/balloon? (All explained later.)

Comparisons to current mortgage interest rates and crowd-funding websites:www.FinancialBananaSplit.com.

Home Buying Basics

It's important to understand home buying basics to prepare for and evaluate your home buying readiness and get the best deal.

There are eight home buying basics to understand before buying a home either as a shareholder or as the sole owner.

1. Legal

A deed in your name(s) equals property/home ownership the same way a title gives you ownership of an automobile.

This gives you specific rights and responsibilities:

- Quiet enjoyment of your property.
- Inviting who you want, when you want, to your house.
- Remodeling, demolition, construction to fit your lifestyle.
- Selling or renting your property and making a profit.
- Paying property taxes. Buying fire and liability insurance.
- Maintaining your home's exterior within locally accepted standards for safety, sanitation, physical appearance, etc.
- Loss of use due to disaster or construction defects.
- Your county clerk will have information on taxes, etc.
- Does a home owners association (HOA) exist? Applicable fees and restrictions?

2. Investment

Owning your own home should be your initial primary financial investment because of all of its financial benefits.

As an investment, your home incorporates many classic investment strategies (detailed in Ingredient Five: Investing):

- Appreciation: Real estate historically increases over time.
- Wealth Creation: You increase your percentage of home ownership with each mortgage payment because this reduces the outstanding principal owed on your mortgage balance (except "interest only" mortgages, explained later.)

- Pay Yourself First: Paying off your mortgage benefits you first, not a landlord.

- Cash Flow: Deductions for mortgage interest, property taxes, home office, etc. all decrease your annual tax bill, adding to your positive cash flow.

- Asset Diversification: Your investments should be "diversified" – put into different "classes" of assets: stocks, bonds, real estate, commodities (oil, corn, gold, soybeans, etc.). This protects your money because, when some asset classes are down, others are up. Your home is your real estate asset.

- Leveraging: Using other people's money to make money. The majority of money for your house purchase is loaned to you by the mortgage lender. You only contribute the down payment cash: 5% to 20%. Example: House purchase price = $200,000. Your down payment = $20,000 (10%). You obtain a mortgage for the other $180,000 (90%). Purchasing a $200,000 house with $20,000 cash is 10:1 leveraging of your money.

3. House Affordability

How much home can you afford to buy and maintain? To obtain a mortgage, you must be able to pay all your basic monthly housing costs, known as PITI – see below.

"PITI" (pronounced pity) covers the house costs of Principal + Interest + Taxes + Insurance. The total should not exceed 28% of your monthly household gross (pre-tax) income. Also, taking a larger loan, even if offered, can and has put people at greater risk of foreclosure, as happened in 2008. Example: Total gross monthly household income = $4,200. Total monthly PITI expenses should not exceed $1,176 (28% of $4,200).

Components of example:

a) $180,000 mortgage @ 3.49% (P+I)/per month = $807.28

b) $3,000 annual property taxes/per month = $250.00

c) $1,200 annual home owner's insurance = $100.00

Total PITI/per month = $1,157.28

In the above example, the monthly income qualifies to buy this house because it's more than the monthly PITI: income of $1,176 versus PITI of $1,157.28.

Your PITI affordability level: www.FinancialBananaSplit.com

4. Affordable Housing

Our nation has an affordable housing crisis due to factors such as lack of supply – only 20% of new housing is classified as affordable (National Association of Home Builders). Luxury apartments are favored by builders. A potential solution for many is the "step up" collaborative home ownership program advocated throughout this book. This works best for those seeking three- to five-year housing partners who want to: buy > profit > move up to sole ownership.

Let's look at the following information:

The average monthly rent for a one-bedroom apartment is $1,057.

Compare this to the previous monthly PITI example. Realizing your own house can give you thousands in income tax deductions every year (equal to your mortgage interest plus property taxes) plus the historical price appreciation of real estate, it's clear owning is a better value than renting.

Additionally, if this house is collaboratively owned by four share-holders, each shareholder's monthly PITI is $289. Compare that to the average one-bedroom apartment rent of $1057 – wow!

That's an even more compelling financial reason to own your own home sooner than later.

This example will be utilized again in Step Three: Collaborate for Wealth Building. That details how to become a homeowner sooner than later (with a little help from your friends).

Other housing-related costs to consider beyond PITI include:

- Utilities: power, water, sewer.
- Internet, television, and phone services.
- Lawn maintenance and snow removal.
- Repairs, maintenance, replacement, improvements as needed
- Private Mortgage Insurance (PMI) if down payment < 20%.

Risks in Home Ownership

No investment is risk free, and home ownership has its own unique risks:

1. Price declines due to economic conditions locally or nationally. You will be most affected if you must sell when prices are much lower than your purchase price. Renting your house or your share in your collaborative house might be your only option until prices appreciate enough to sell.

2. The house is uninhabitable, temporarily or permanently, due to damage from a natural disaster, mold, or structural failure. You're still liable for mortgage payments and real estate taxes. Insurance might pay for all or part of your loss. You'll need to temporarily or permanently relocate.

Take these risks into consideration, as well as all the benefits of home ownership, and try to determine your probable future scenario before making this major life commitment.

Buying a home at a price close to its historic low rather than its historic high with a mortgage you can afford can significantly reduce your financial risks and improve your investment prospects. Methods for calculating these are covered later in this book.

5. The Mortgage

The Federal Truth In Lending Act (TILA) requires your lender to give you two documents itemizing all mortgage financing costs: Initial: Loan Estimate Form (3 pages). Final: Closing Disclosure Form (5 pages). Samples: FinancialBananaSplit.com.

Your best choice for financing is the standard 30-year fixed-rate mortgage loaned at a competitive interest rate. This is because the mortgage payment is fixed and can never go higher, giving predictability to your monthly payments. It also has the advantage of going lower if you choose to refinance when interest rates decline. It's the gold standard for a reasonably affordable mortgage.

Note: Be aware, **refinancing** a mortgage means starting over with a **full new mortgage term**. Prepaying your current mortgage in a shorter time rather than refinancing might be a smarter choice and might also save thousands in additional interest. See example below.

Verify there is no prepayment penalty. Then you can make extra principal payments when you have extra cash. Your own fully paid-off residence is generally the smartest investment you can make. Why? Live where you don't own, and you're paying someone else's mortgage and taxes for their property.

Example: House price of $200,000 with mortgage of $180,000 @ 3.49%: 30 year mortgage total cost = $290,621. If paid off in 20 years, total cost = $250,932.

This early pay-off is done by paying an extra $230 per month towards the mortgage. That's a $39,689 savings in interest payments.

Once your mortgage is paid off, cash flow greatly increases. Your credit rating, down payment amount, and income all determine what interest rate, points, and type (fixed/variable/blend) of mortgage you'll be offered.

Caution: If you don't qualify for the standard fixed-rate 30- year mortgage, be wary of accepting other types of mortgages, as they involve higher risk.

Example: The "interest only" mortgage. Your monthly mortgage payments are low because they only go towards paying the interest expense on the mortgage, not principal.

The risk with this type of mortgage is that eventually you have to pay off or refinance it, typically in five or ten years, in one lump sum known as a "balloon" payment. If you don't have the cash or don't qualify to refinance your principal, you could lose your home in a court-ordered foreclosure.

A Reverse Mortgage

The reverse mortgage program buys your home if you're 62 years of age or older and meet certain criteria.

Positives: You can reside in your home until death. You receive a cash lump-sum, line-of-credit or income stream. Negatives: The mortgage company sells your home upon death, you receive a below-market price for your home to fund your "cash-out," high fees, and complicated contract. Www.FinancilBananaSplit.com for lenders.

"Rent-to-Own"

Rent-to-own is a structure where part of your rent money is allocated by your landlord towards the purchase of the house. You need to be aware of price relative to comparable homes in the neighborhood, fees, penalties, percentage of your rent allocated to ownership, mortgage interest rate, duration of this process, and proof landlord owns the house (deed/county records).

6. Location

The famous question in real estate is: What are the three most important factors in real estate? Answer: Location, location, location. The "real" in real estate is land ownership. Land is generally the biggest variable in your home's price.

The same house in San Francisco, California, or Wichita, Kansas, will sell for very different prices. Location also determines your home's future value. Besides a luxury location, the next best thing is a house with great future price appreciation due to urban renewal by government or "gentrification" (older houses being torn down and replaced by new homes, condos, new businesses moving into the area), growth in the surrounding area, etc.

Check your county clerk's office, local real estate agencies, and www.FinancialBananaSplit.com for the area's recent price appreciation, proposed development, etc.

Location also factors into the "livability" – quality of life – aspects of your house, such as distance, ease, and cost of travel to work, schools, hospitals, transportation, recreation, shopping, places of worship, air quality, noise, etc.

A must do for anyone considering buying a home is to take a walk around the neighborhood six blocks in every direction from the house at different times of day and night to get a feel for where you'll be making this big investment of time and money. Would you be comfortable living there? Neighborhood changing for better? Worse? Imagine driving up to your house.

7. Type/Physical Condition

Housing type: Decide which type of dwelling design best fits your current and anticipated future needs, including room for an expanding or extended family.

Elements include:

- Overall square footage
- Number of bedrooms and bathrooms, as well as number of levels and number of stairs to climb.
- Is there a basement/attic/garage? How big is the yard, if any? A larger yard equals higher taxes and maintenance.
- Physical condition: Before you buy, it's advisable to hire a professional home inspector and obtain, in writing, a report detailing the home's total physical condition. Structural, mold, or other damage could cost tens of thousands of dollars to repair.
- Is the house connected to the town sewer and water, or does it have its own well and septic system? What is the condition of the well and septic system? Repairs needed?
- Ask your inspector for cost estimates of planned remodeling.

"Sweat equity" is when you do improvements to the house yourself to save money without hiring professionals. Be realistic about your available time and skill level.

Check with your town if permits are required for electrical, plumbing, or other renovations.

8. Intention and Timing

Intention: Buying a home is a serious commitment. What is your intention for this purchase? Long-term living? Investment? Rental property? Work space?

A basic rule: Don't buy a home as a residence (as opposed to an investment) unless you'll live there at least five years.

Why? Every time you move, you pay moving, furniture, mortgage costs, decorating, landscaping, renovations, etc. And you need time for it all. If you're buying a home to "flip" for profit or investment, go to www.FinancialBananaSplit.com for additional resources. All the basic rules of home buying apply to house flipping: comparative pricing, timing, location, cost to renovate.

Timing: Major economic cycles (bad > good > bad) occur about every 12 years. Be aware of where we are in the economic cycle to avoid buying in a housing "bubble" – paying too much for a house because of temporary unrealistic or unsupportable market conditions.

Clues? Mortgages given to anyone even with poor credit and no down payment requirements. Housing bubbles also include not enough houses for sale to meet buyer demand. This causes bidding wars for houses above asking price.

If houses in the neighborhood you're considering have risen in price 50% or more over the past five years, talk to homeowners to determine if there is any realistic reason for this dramatic price increase. If there isn't and a crash seems inevitable, be smart and wait. Remember the classic rule: Buy low, sell high.

Paying way too much for housing due to market conditions, unanticipated costly repairs, or any other reason can quickly turn your American Dream into your American Nightmare. Www.FinancialBananaSplit.com for housing market information.

True Story – Sacrifice

While I was operating a nursing home, I started a healthcare staffing agency with a nurse business partner in the 1990s.

We recruited nurses from overseas who wanted to save as much money as possible in order to buy a home in their native country. This required that they pay as little rent as possible while working in the United States.

We rented several two-bedroom apartments (eight nurses could share on different shift schedules) and placed two bunk beds in each bedroom. It was close, but comfortable.

By sharing an apartment, each nurse only had to pay $100 of the $800 rent per month. The nurses were able to budget, limit living expenses, and send money "back home" to purchase their own homes.

Moral of the story: Sacrifice succeeds!

Ingredient Two – Conclusion

Home Ownership gives you the right to say: "There's no place like home." Work towards owning a home of your own, smartly, by understanding and applying the information presented in this Ingredient.

4

Ingredient Three: Loans, Credit, and Debt

Loans, credit, and debt are the ice cream in the banana split. Ways to use money are as numerous as ice cream flavors.

"Beware of little expenses, a small leak will sink a great ship."

(Benjamin Franklin, American statesman, 18th century)

If your credit charges are never fully paid off, they can grow into unmanageable, life-wrecking debt as interest and penalties accumulate.

Avoid this scenario. Use loans, credit, and debt to your financial advantage by understanding what they are, how they work, and how to best manage them. Student loans are a huge issue to many. I explain how to pay off much of this debt using the equity in your home later in the book.

Loan Basics – Definitions

One of the best ways to keep debt under control is to understand how your loan works. This includes credit card debt and how much it actually costs to repay the money you've borrowed.

Definitions of loan terms and documents are explained below:

- **Credit:** Amount of money you're qualified to borrow and that requires repayment.
- **Debt:** Amount of money you've borrowed and requires repayment. Credit turns into debt as soon as it's used.
- **Creditor:** A lender you owe money to such as a bank, credit card company, etc.
- **Principal:** Amount borrowed equal to the purchase price of the item bought.
- **Interest:** Amounts paid by you to the lender for the use of their money, usually expressed as a percentage (%) of the principal (amount borrowed).

The lender will use one of two methods to calculate your loan's interest expense:

1. **Simple interest:** Interest charged only on a loan's outstanding principal balance.
2. **Compound interest:** Interest charged on a loan's outstanding principal balance plus interest charged on the loan's outstanding interest. Compounding can be daily/ monthly/quarterly/ annually. The loan states the frequency.

Compound interest is more expensive than simple interest.

The cost difference between simple and compound interest loans is illustrated as follows:

Example: Loan amount: $30,000/stated interest rate: 6%/ loan duration: 20 years. Simple interest loan – Total interest cost: $21,583 Compound interest loan – Total interest cost: $28,002.

The compound interest loan costs $6,419 more over the life of the loan than the simple interest loan even though both loans have the same stated interest rate and duration.

The "stated" interest rate is the pure interest rate. It doesn't factor in fees, charges or compound interest.

Total interest costs must legally be disclosed on the Truth in Lending Statement (see below).

- **APR** (annual percentage rate): All costs of a loan, including fees, compound interest expenses, and other charges, are converted into a simple interest rate known as the APR. This makes it easier to compare the true costs of various loans. In the example above, the two loans were both offered at the stated interest rate of 6%, but because of the compounding feature in the second loan, its APR would have been shown as 8% on a Truth In Lending Statement.

- **Loan Disclosure Statement:** A lender must disclose all costs and features of a loan on a Loan Disclosure Statement, per federal law. It details loan amount, interest rate – including APR – loan duration, frequency and amount of payments, interest calculation – simple or compound – total interest cost over the life of the loan, fees, costs, and penalties, and how they're triggered. Read, understand, and sign only if you can make all payments. Defaulting on a loan can severely damage your credit. Damaged credit prevents you from obtaining loans, credit cards, a mortgage, renting an apartment, even employment. FinancialBananaSplit.com for Loan Disclosure sample.

- **Secured Debt:** This is when property is pledged as "collateral" (security) to obtain a loan. If you fail to repay the loan, the lender can repossess the collateral. This is usually associated with a mortgage (house loan) or car loan, both of which are assets (things of value).

- **Unsecured Debt:** This is when no property is pledged to obtain a loan. If you fail to repay the loan, the lender can sue you, causing bankruptcy. This is common with credit card debt. A credit card is actually a debt card: It loans you money with interest. The credit used turns into your debt.

Credit

Your credit in the financial world is your reputation, your trustworthiness. It's affected, good and bad, by your actions or damaged by the actions of others, most commonly identity theft.

Let's look at each of these in more detail:

Your Actions

Positive actions affecting your credit:

- Paying bills on time, avoiding late charges and penalties.
- Not using more than 30% of the credit limit on any credit card routinely.
- Using a debit card instead of a credit card for purchases. This keeps your average monthly credit balance low.

Negative actions affecting your credit:

- Not paying bills on time. Incurring late charges and penalties.
- Failure to repay a loan (defaulting).
- Declaring bankruptcy in court.
- Routinely using more than 30% of the credit limit on any credit card.

You need to balance offers of cash back and points against how it might lower your credit score.

True Story – Credit Card

Shortly before I started research for this book, I asked my credit card issuer if they would increase my credit limit. They denied my request because my FICO score was in the low 600s. I couldn't believe it!!

I thought that because I had several million dollars invested through the same bank that had issued my credit card, I wouldn't be denied. I was wrong.

After learning the same information presented to you in this book, I took the following steps to raise my FICO score:

- I used my debit card for purchases instead of my credit card.
- I requested my credit records from the three credit bureaus and found an old loan that I was being billed for monthly that I had forgotten about. It wasn't huge, so I paid it off in full.
- There was a recurring charge on my monthly credit card statement for a service I no longer used. I cancelled it.

After taking these three simple steps, my FICO score improved to 823, which is in the "perfect" credit range. Several months later, when I applied for my business credit card, the bank granted me double the standard credit limit due in part to my high personal credit score. I realized I didn't need more credit. I needed to be smarter with the credit I already had.

Identity Theft

Your financial identity can be attacked and stolen by criminals who use your credit to make unauthorized purchases. This is damaging to your credit and life. Take these steps to monitor, prevent, and repair identity theft:

- Never give your social security number to anyone on the internet or to anyone else unless they can be verified and trusted and their use of your social security number is limited to a specific purpose, in writing.
- Shred all documents with personal financial information before you discard them.
- Don't open or click on internet links or files unless you trust the source.
- Federal law permits you to review your credit reports for free from each of the three credit reporting agencies, Experian, Equifax, and Transunion, once per year.

Use these services to verify the amounts and current status (amounts outstanding, payment due date, etc.) for all debts, including credit cards, car loans, mortgages, etc.

Free credit check sites and links to credit monitoring services which help you avoid being a victim of credit fraud can be found at www.FinancialBananaSplit.com

If you spot problems, take steps to resolve them immediately. Contact the credit card company, bank, or other debt issuer and address the problem with relevant documents (see below):

If your identity has been stolen, follow these steps:

1. Place a fraud alert on your credit by calling: (800) 685-1111. This prevents any more charges to your credit card.
2. File a police report at your local police station.
3. Create an identity theft report: www.consumer.ftc.gov/topics/ repairingidentity-theft.com.
4. To fix the fraud, contact the fraud departments of all affected businesses and credit agencies using the above reports as evidence.

Your Credit Score: FICO

Your credit rating is based on your "FICO" score, a number from 300 to 850. As a direct result of your FICO score, your cost to finance (borrow money) can vary greatly.

Example: A $20,000 car loan for 48 months using different credit scores and their costs is illustrated below:

FICO Score	Credit Rating	Interest Rate	Monthly Payment	Interest Expense	Total Cost
720–850	Excellent	3%	$442.69	$1248.95	$21,248.95
690–719	Great	4%	$451.56	$1675.89	$21,675.89
670–689	Very Good	5%	$460.59	$2108.17	$22,108.12
650–669	Good	7%	$478.92	$2988.39	$22,988.12
630–649	Fair	10%	$507.25	$4348.08	$24,348.08
610–629	Poor	12%	$526.68	$5280.48	$25,280.48
580–609	Very Poor	15%	$556.61	$6717.52	$26,717.52

The difference in the cost of the car between an "excellent" and a "very poor" credit rating is over five thousand dollars.

Your credit rating affects interest rates and your ability to qualify for a mortgage or credit cards and might even have a negative impact on your ability to rent housing or secure employment.

Check your credit rating: www.FinancialBananaSplit.com

Establishing Credit

Establishing credit is an important step to take in order to create wealth on your path to economic security. Credit allows you to obtain a mortgage to buy a house, which, when paid off, significantly reduces your living expenses and greatly increases your cash flow.

There are several basic ways to establish credit:

- Put rent, utilities, and internet services in your name. Pay them on time, every month. Late payments will result in a lowered "FICO" score, so keep your payments current.
- Open and maintain a bank checking account. This proves you can manage money and provides documentation to lenders. Find one with no minimum balance fee.
- Obtain a financial institution credit card such as VISA/Discover/MasterCard. You can choose a "standard" credit limit, where the bank will set your limit based on your FICO score and income. Or you can choose a "secured" limit, where you give a deposit to your bank. Your credit limit is this amount.

Controlling Debt

After you've established credit, here's how to stay out of debt:

- Make a monthly budget to be aware of your cash flow. (See Ingredient One: Cash Flow and Banking.)
- Don't charge more than you can pay back every month.
- Treat your credit card like cash: Set up an automatic deduction from your checking account to pay the full amount of all of your credit card charges every month.
- You can use a credit card as little as once every three months for 20 dollars' worth of purchases. This will maintain or even increase your FICO score. It's best to limit its use to emergencies other than the small charge to maintain it. Know your credit card interest rate, penalties, and fees as stated in the credit card agreement, which is a contract.
- Check your bank and credit card statements every month for accuracy, including purchases you didn't make, fees, interest charges, and overcharges.

- Get a debit card from your bank at the same time you get a credit card. With a debit card, money is deducted directly from your checking account the same as a cash payment would be, instead of it going onto your credit card balance. This avoids interest piling up as well as penalties and late fees if you don't fully pay off your credit card(s) totals monthly.

- Pay bills on time to avoid late charges and penalties that will lower your credit rating. Set up automatic monthly bill paying with your bank for recurring charges (rent/utilities/loans, etc.). Make sure you have enough money in your checking account at all times to cover these withdrawals. Ask your bank for their app to check balances using your mobile phone.

- Don't exceed 30% of credit card limits on a regular basis.

- No new debt is the smartest choice for your financial health.

- Cash back, rewards, and free point programs are a tempting incentive to open multiple credit card accounts. Do this only if you can pay off every credit card every month, not use more than 30% of your allowed credit on any card, have plenty of extra cash to pay all debts if you lose your job, and make sure your credit score never drops below 670. Then you might chance having multiple credit cards.

Paying off and staying out of debt is the formula for a successful financial future.

A high debt translates into a lower FICO score and higher borrowing costs. This could mean the difference between qualifying for a mortgage or not and potentially having to file for bankruptcy due to insurmountable debt.

Paying Down Debt Burden – Two Methods

Both methods get you out of debt. The "smart" method might be best if you have a loan with interest exceeding 10%, which is very costly.

Quick Pay-off Method

- Make a list of all debts and their amounts, smallest at the top, largest on the bottom.
- Pay the minimum amount due on all debts.
- Use any extra cash to pay off the smallest debt first.
- When the smallest debt is paid off, do the same for the next debt on your list until it's paid off, and so on, until finished.
- Don't accumulate any new debt until your list is finished. No new debt is the smartest choice for your financial health.

Smart Pay-off Method

- Make a list of all debts with their interest rates, highest interest rate at the top, lowest rate on the bottom.
- Pay the minimum due on all debts.
- Use any extra cash to pay off the debt with the highest interest rate first.
- When that one is paid off, do the same for the next debt on your list until it's paid off, and so on, until finished.
- Don't accumulate any new debt until your list is finished. No new debt is the smartest choice for your financial health.

Debt Consolidation

This technique combines multiple loans into a single, lower-interest loan with lower monthly payments. Collateral is usually required. These loans are typically for a second mortgage or a home equity line of credit. You're putting your house at risk of foreclosure if you default on this loan.

First, contact your creditors to see if they will work with you. Don't accumulate new debt until this loan is paid off. No new debt is the smartest choice for your financial health.

See www.FinancialBananaSplit.com for lender websites.

Credit Counseling

These services offer customized plans to get you out of debt, including budget planning. They work with your creditors to try to extend/forgive/rewrite all or part of your debt to a lower monthly amount you can manage to pay.

You can also call individual creditors first to see if they will work with you. www.FinancialBananaSplit.com for credit counseling services. This list only includes free, non-profit organizations.

Student Loans/Home Equity Loan

I advocate home ownership because "free cash" (due to your home increasing in value) can ease debt burden as follows:

- The average student loan balance is $30,000.
- The average interest rate on this debt is 6.8%.
- The current interest rate on a home equity loan is 4.75% – much less than the student loan rate.

If your home is worth more today than when you purchased it, that value difference can be used as loan collateral to obtain a home equity loan – a second mortgage on your home. Note: Defaulting can cause home loss due to foreclosure.

If you use home equity proceeds to pay off student debt, you'll be able to:

1. Pay back the home equity loan in less time because the same amount of money pays more debt due to its lower interest rate.

2. Pay back the home equity loan for much less interest expense than the student loan due to its lower interest rate.

Example: Student loan $30,000/interest rate 6.8% for 20 years. Monthly payment $229. Total interest expense = $24,960. Home equity loan $30,000/interest rate 4.75% for 20 years. Monthly payment $192. Total interest expense = $16,134.

The difference in interest costs of $8,826 between these two types of loans is huge! Total payback amounts: student loan $54,960 vs. home equity loan $46,134. Why pay more for the same thing?

It pays to get and stay on the path to the American Dream. In other words: Get ye into home ownership.

If you can't take advantage of a home equity loan to pay off your student loan, consider other options and ask your lender about forbearance and deferment. These options allow you to postpone loan payments: deferment, without accruing interest, and forbearance, while still accruing interest. A job during college lets you pay off student debt as it happens.

True Story – College Job

My parents and grandparents were able to pay my college tuition, but any extra spending money I had to earn myself.

I got a job as the delivery person for a local florist near my school in Washington, DC. It was used by many prominent politicians as well as wealthy people in the DC area.

As I was the regular delivery person, I had the opportunity to see inside many mansions, including one where former Secretary of State Henry Kissinger would be a dinner guest. I also delivered flowers to the infamous Watergate Hotel where Republican operatives, allegedly with the knowledge of then President Nixon, broke into the Democrats' campaign headquarters to steal information (two years before my time).

This incident was depicted in a famous movie when the main character (Forest) sees flashlights moving inside a Washington DC hotel room and calls the front desk to investigate.

My best delivery memories were when I'd walk into a hospital waiting room with a huge bouquet of flowers (destined for a VIP patient), and everybody (patients, staff, visitors) would light up like Fourth of July fireworks.

Moral of the story: Get a job. Do good. You never know what positive adventures and memories await.

Debt Burden: Impossible

Bad things happen when you're unable to pay debts. It can make your life a horror show when you're unable to obtain credit cards, car loans, student loans, or buy a house. You can also be turned down for jobs, apartment rentals, utilities, cell phones, and even dates. Yes, a date might ask to see your credit score on your phone – before committing to a more serious relationship.

Bad credit requiring legal action tells the world you're a loser. Don't be a loser. Learn these techniques to avoid loserville. To keep bad things from happening, it's all about being aware of your cash flow: inflow versus outflow. This means not spending more than you take in each month.

93

What are the biggest expenses in your life?

Student loans? Technology? Debt? Clothes? Entertainment? Want another tattoo? Get it the first day you move into your own home. That's one even your parents won't object to. You are the parent? Want to retire but can't yet? Both of you need to:

1. Complete your monthly budget on page 59.
2. Follow this book's path to the American Dream.

Financial Bad Stuff To Avoid

Collection Agencies

Collection agencies are hired by creditors to collect debt. They report their progress/status to the credit bureaus. Non-payment can lead to a lowering of your FICO score and a bad credit rating.

If you're contacted by a collection agency, take these steps:

- Ask the collection agency to send written proof of all debts.
- Write them a "cease and desist" letter and send it by certified mail. This ends the collection agency's right to keep contacting you for the same debt, although they can continue other actions: FICO reporting, legal action, paycheck garnishment, etc.

(See sample letter: www.FinancialBananaSplit.com). Verify your debts by contacting your creditors and making arrangements to pay them off as soon as possible.

Bankruptcy

Bankruptcy is a legal process filed by you or on your behalf in court to give you protection from creditors while you plan and settle (or have dismissed) unpayable debts.

The two most common forms of personal bankruptcy are:

- Chapter 7 Bankruptcy: Liquidation of assets to permanently discharge debts. Assets to be sold: House, car, boat, jewelry, savings, etc. Debts that cannot be discharged: Taxes, mortgages, student loans, alimony, child support, and medical bills. Once a debt is discharged through Chapter 7, it is gone forever.
- Chapter 13 Bankruptcy: Reorganization and repayment. You are required to make court-ordered payments to creditors. Selling of assets is optional. The court decides payment schedule.

Bankruptcy makes it difficult to re-establish full credit for seven years. To fix, read Establishing Credit, on page 87. You can file for bankruptcy using an attorney, a non-attorney bankruptcy petition preparer, or bankruptcy software. These services have different costs and levels of accuracy. Contact the county clerk, state BAR (lawyers) association, or www.FinancialBananaSplit.com for resources.

Foreclosure

Foreclosure is a legal process where you lose your home due to your inability to pay your mortgage.
- You are court ordered to vacate your home (sheriff notified).
- All credit cards are cancelled.
- You can re-establish your credit by following Establishing Credit on page 87. Mortgages take seven years to requalify.

Ingredient Three - Conclusion

You can keep on the path to the American Dream if you understand cash flow, follow your budget, and use loans/credit/debt to strengthen, not weaken, your financial life.

5

Ingredient Four:
Avoiding Financial Landmines

Avoiding Financial Landmines are the banana split toppings, covering other Ingredients and affecting their overall flavor.

Certain basics need to be included in your financial planning to avoid paying unforeseen legal costs, fees, penalties, etc.

Protect your money by following the guidelines outlined below for income taxes, contracts, insurance, dealing with documents, and estate planning.

Income Taxes

"In this world nothing is certain except death and taxes."
(Benjamin Franklin, American statesman, 1789)

Income taxes are the only taxes you've got to actively compute every year. Once done, you'll pay either less in taxes or receive a bigger refund for taxes paid than if you hadn't made the effort. Ignoring this can result in property seizure, bankruptcy, bad credit, and even jail for fraud.

You can minimize your taxes and stay out of trouble by following these income tax basics.

Use the Correct Income Tax Return

Which income tax return (form) to file depends on your needs. Use the correct return so you pay the least in taxes.

Example: Natalie earned $40,000 from a full-time job this year. She made a pension contribution and had interest expenses from her student loan. The examples below illustrate the difference that using the proper income tax return can make in reducing your income tax liability:

Most tax liability:	*Least tax liability:*
Files 1040EZ return	Files 1040A return
Gross income: $40,000	Gross income: $40,000
Adjusted gross income: $40,000	Pension contribution: $5,000
	Student loan interest: $3,000
Tax rate for this income 25%	Adjusted gross income: $32,000
	Tax rate for this income: 15%
Tax before standard	Tax before standard
adjustments: $10,000.	adjustments: $4,800.

Natalie's taxable income decreased $5,200 using the correct tax return, because the 1040A allows deductions, This put her income in a lower tax bracket (rate).

Determine which income tax return minimizes your taxes:

- 1040EZ – Income below $100,000, no dependents, interest income less than $1,500, no deductions (no interest on student loans, no pension contribution, etc.).
- 1040A – Income below $100,000, not self-employed, limited deductions (mortgage, pension, student loan interest).

- 1040 – Income over $100,000, self-employed, itemized deductions exceed standard deductions (paid property taxes, large charitable contributions, large medical expenses, etc.).

See the Maintaining Documents section below for which documents to keep for what time period to support tax filing.

The government can audit you for up to three years after you file a tax return, forever if they suspect fraud. There are several ways to file, including paper, e-mail, etc.

Sources are available to help you prepare your income tax return. Go to: www.FinancialBananaSplit.com for links to the IRS website and tax preparation services.

Income Tax – Basic Definitions

Know these basic definitions to understand income taxes:

- Income Tax – A tax on your earnings collected by a government (federal/state/city). Example: Federal income tax is collected annually by the IRS (Internal Revenue Service).
- Income Tax Rate – A percentage of income used to calculate income taxes owed.
- Taxable Earnings – Income received from jobs, tips, investments, rents, gifts, etc.
- Taxpayer – A resident of the United States earning over $10,300 annually (subject to change).
- Income Tax Deduction – Amount deducted from income to reduce taxes owed. Examples: Pension contribution, student loan interest, property taxes, mortgage interest, etc.
- Income Tax Credit – Amount deducted from your total tax liability, which reduces taxes owed. Examples: Earned income tax credit and solar tax credit.

- Personal Tax Exemption – An amount allowed by the IRS, deducted from income, that reduces taxes owed. Example: Standard exemption for single taxpayers is $4,000.
- Tax Filing – Submitting your tax return to the government. Example: 1040EZ/1040A/1040.
- Filing Deadline – Date income tax return due. Example: Federal returns are due every April 15th for individuals.
- Tax Year: Year for which taxes are due. Example: Calendar year for individuals is Jan.–Dec.
- Income Documentation: Documents showing earnings during the tax year. Examples: W-2 wage statement, 1099 bank interest, and investment income.
- Deduction Documentation: Documents showing qualified (as allowed by the IRS or state of residence) expense or loss. Examples: Medical bills, loan interest documents, charity receipts, pension contributions, etc.

Contracts

Contracts are legally binding documents. All signors to the contract are obligated to comply with all terms and conditions or pay costs, incur legal fees, or receive a lowered credit rating for non-compliance, etc.

* READ THE ENTIRE CONTRACT BEFORE SIGNING *

Don't sign any contract until you can
identify, understand, and agree to all terms and conditions.

Check all contracts (phone service, mortgage, car loan, gym membership, rental housing, car rental, etc.) for the following 10 elements (not all apply to all contracts) as follows:

A Contract – 10 Elements

1. Payment: What will you pay, or what will you be paid? Minimum, maximum, weekly, monthly, total, etc.

2. Non-compliance: Are there consequences? Penalties, charges, obligations?

3. Termination: Automatically ends or renews? Notice given? By whom?

4. Duration of contract: Specific time frame or open-ended?

5. Performance: What is required specifically of you and the seller (gym, phone company, landlord, car lease) to be done?

6. Returns: Items need to be returned when, how, and in what condition? Penalties?

7. Assignment: Is the contract "assignable" (transferrable to others) by you or seller? Any additional charges?

8. Buy option: Available? When? Price, fees, taxes, other conditions?

9. Getting the best deal: Receiving all applicable discounts, rebates, competitor's coupons, trade-ins, etc.?

10. Insurance: Who pays for property damage, liability (injury to persons) insurance?

Once you've identified all applicable elements in your contract, preference choices need to be made: color, etc. Doubts? Contact county clerk and legal or financial help before signing. Sample contract at www.FinancialBananaSplit.com.

Every contract has its own order of important elements. Look through the contract for each element.

To help you review a contract, follow this sequence:

1. Start by reading Element 1: Payment. Find and identify payment-related terms and conditions throughout the contract.

2. Do you understand and agree to what is being asked or stated in the contract? If YES, move on to step three below. If NO, ask questions and/or negotiate (see this book's Step One: Self-awareness – Negotiation). If you still don't understand or can't accept the contract terms and conditions or revisions, don't sign it. Walk away. You have my permission.

3. Can you accept all contract terms and conditions in this element?

If YES, repeat these steps for elements two through ten.

True Story – Former Boss

My former boss was an old school bookkeeper who was always being marketed to by young, smart, college-educated, smooth-talking salespeople.

They presented their sales pitch in a complex manner, hoping to mask reality and that she was too intimidated by lack of understanding to ask questions and just accept and sign.

One day, I was in her office and witnessed a sales pitch. She kept asking questions and couldn't understand the full consequences of buying this particular product (hand soap dispensers).

Instead of being intimidated, feeling stupid, or signing the contract, she simply said, "I can't buy something I don't understand. Come back when you can explain it to me better."

In other words, she wasn't the problem; the salesperson was. If he couldn't explain something in terms that were understandable to her, he was the one who was ignorant. You do the same. If you can't repeat to the salesperson exactly what the product or service is they're selling, don't sign the contract.

Insurance

The purpose of insurance is to protect your assets from being sold to pay for losses. Damage to things is **property** loss. Injury or death to a person is **liability**. This includes legal, medical, and other costs.

A "deductible" is the amount you pay for losses before the insurance company pays. The higher the deductible, the lower your insurance policy "premium" (cost to buy) should be.

How much insurance coverage do you need? A general rule is to buy the amount of insurance that protects your assets (savings/car/house, etc.) from having to be sold to pay claims, which could leave you broke and possibly filing for bankruptcy.

Different insurance types and coverages are explained below:

- Renter's Insurance – Coverage needs to pay for injury to you and others (liability) while in your apartment and replacement of belongings (property) in case they are destroyed or stolen. Example: You fail to purchase renter's insurance for your apartment. A friend visits. She slips and falls on your wet kitchen floor, injuring herself, requiring hospitalization with $19,000 in medical bills. She sues you and your landlord. You lose in court and are ordered to pay. Now you have to empty your savings account of its entire $5,000 and sell your car to get an additional $14,000 to comply with the court order. Inexpensive renter's insurance ($150 per year?) would have covered this, and the insurance company would have defended you in court.

- Auto Insurance – Liability coverage pays for injury to others. Medical and Personal Injury Protection coverage pays your medical expenses. Collision and Comprehensive coverage pays for vehicle damage.

- Healthcare Insurance – Coverage needs to pay for all medical costs and continuing care for all persons included in the policy. It's expensive. It's a huge benefit if paid by your employer.
- House Insurance – Coverage needs to pay for fire damage, damage caused by acts of nature common in your area (hurricanes, fire, flood, etc.), and injury to persons in your house or on your property (liability insurance) – the same injury consequences as renters insurance above.
- Life Insurance – Pays upon the death of the insured. Coverage should have a death benefit big enough to support loved ones who depend on your financial support to pay mortgage costs, health bills, education, and living costs for the time needed.

There are two main types of life insurance: term and whole life.

Term life insurance: Low annual cost. No coverage if you stop paying. Coverage is for a specified number of years. Renewal is necessary after the term ends, at which point, you'll need to requalify, probably at a higher rate because you're older.

Whole life insurance: Once you buy a policy, renewal is not necessary unless you fail to pay premiums before the policy "self-funds"(the policy earns annual dividends equal to or greater than the annual premium). Coverage lasts until your death regardless of your health status. You can borrow the "cash value" in your policy, which increases over time, as premiums are paid. The policy can increase in value over time, similar to an investment.

I believe you should, as a minimum, purchase an inexpensive term life insurance policy on your life if there is anyone who depends or will depend on you financially (wife/children/ partner). This will replace your lost income for them.

Or, if no one depends on you financially but you want to throw an unforgettable New Orleans/Mardi Gras-style funeral party when you die, it'll only happen if you leave enough money for that event plus a big tip for the person who's to arrange it all.

Whole life insurance is wise to purchase when you have extra money – an automatic deduction is great to set up – because it's paid off in about 15 years, it continues to grow even in a bad economy, and you're always covered no matter your health or age. You can start small ($50,000?) and can always buy more.

True Story – My Whole Life Insurance

I currently own several million dollars of fully paid up – and growing – whole life insurance policies with Mass Mutual.

I purchased my first million-dollar whole life insurance policy when I was 33 years old. I paid $20,000 for 14 years – total payments of $280K. My death benefit is 400% larger than my cost. I was single, I started making good money, and I figured someday I'd have a family who would depend on me, if not emotionally (ha ha) at least financially.

Even through periods of historically low interest rates and economic downturns, my whole life policies have continued to pay dividends of between five and eight percent.

The dividends earned on these policies now completely pay for my annual insurance premiums plus purchase additional insurance.

If you do choose to purchase a whole life insurance policy, verify the issuing insurance company is highly rated and has been in business for at least twenty years (Mass Mutual has been around for 150+ years).

Links to life insurance company websites and policy information: www.FinancialBananaSplit.com

Moral of the Story

Planning for the future now, when things are generally cheaper, pays off.

Dealing with Documents

You need to retain certain documents to prove an event occurred, taxes were paid, repairs were done, items were purchased, donations were made, etc.

The IRS has the right to audit you going back three years . . . forever if they suspect fraud.

It's reasonable to keep all documents related to major purchases – life insurance, auto, appliances, electronics, etc., for at least seven years or longer if a warranty exists.

Common documents to retain include:

- Bank and securities statements, documents showing income, tax returns, wage and property tax statements.
- Birth certificate, passport, driver's license, social security card, automobile title, etc.
- Insurance policies, warranties, repair receipts, medical expenses.
- Charity and purchase receipts, registrations, manuals, deeds.

Store them in a secure, dry, and accessible place.

Your system can be as simple as keeping all documents for the same year in a plastic folder in a locked, fireproof cabinet.

The importance of document retention is multiplied when you have collaborative ownership (Step Three: Collaborate for Wealth

Building). People count on you, and you count on them to be able to offer documented proof events occurred.

Original signed and dated documents offer the best proof. As added protection, take pictures and store data electronically.

Estate Planning

Your estate is created (after death) from your assets, including cash, securities, real estate, life insurance proceeds, jewelry, other personal assets, etc. You need a will and revocable trust. Your estate will be controlled, distributed, and assessed large fees by your state's probate court (and its attorneys) unless you have a revocable trust, as explained below:

Will: Your entire estate goes into probate court. You can name an "executor"(financially settles your estate – court not obligated to obey) and appoint a guardian for your minor children. The court decides who gets what and when, including hearing petitions from relatives or others, and it decides guardianship.

Revocable Trust: The assets in this trust avoid probate court. You name an executor to distribute your estate according to your wishes. Guardianship of minor children is still decided by the court. All major assets should be put into this trust. Minor assets and personal effects are distributed according to your will. You can modify or cancel a revocable trust at any time. www.FinancialBananaSplit.com for estate planning websites.

These documents can be prepared by an attorney or online.

Ingredient Four – Conclusion

"The devil is in the details" is a German proverb cautioning us to examine things closely to discover and avoid potential major problems and not rely on surface appearances.

This is the purpose of Avoiding Financial Landmines: to protect your money by understanding and implementing basics whose cost is small relative to what you've got to lose.

6

Ingredient Five: Investing for Wealth and Retirement

Investing is the whipped cream in the banana split. Rapid growth showcases your determination to follow financial plans and quickens your pace towards the American Dream.

Hierarchy of Money Flow
(Where to Target Your Money)

1. Your Home – mortgage payoff or saving for a first home.
2. Retirement – pension investments.
3. Retirement – non-pension investments.
4. Non-Retirement – monies you can afford to lose.

Implementing automatic deductions for the first three targets increases the probability you'll achieve financial success because, if you don't have the cash to spend, you won't spend it. It's basic "out of sight, out of mind" psychology. It works!

First Target Area – Your Home

The first target to aim your money at is your home or saving for your first home (collaborative or sole ownership) because a fully paid-for home is the foundation of financial security.

Your home is also your initial and primary investment because home price appreciation is a fundamental component of wealth creation (Ingredient Two).

All your basic costs of home ownership – principal + interest + taxes + insurance (PITI) – must be fully paid for every month to avoid foreclosure. If you're saving for a home, fund the two future home items in your monthly budget by adding these to your savings account.

This is done before funding investments and pension(s) unless your employer matches pension contributions (see below).

Second Target Area – Pension(s)

The second target to aim your money at is your pension plan. This money grows tax free, stimulating growth. Matching funds from your employer (if offered) is effectively free money (see pension details below).

Third Target Area – Investments

The third target to aim your money at is your non-pension investments. Income and gains generated are taxable when earned, but choosing solid investments and then reinvesting earnings back into these investments supercharges financial growth.

Fourth Target Area – Funny Bone

The fourth target to aim your money at is your funny bone. It's for enjoying and maybe learning something – about money and yourself.

I. **Pension Plans**
   II. **Investing:**
      a) **Securities**
      b) **Principles**
      c) **Strategies**
      III. **Retirement Planning**

You need to understand your pension plan options – (I) the types of pensions and how they work, (II) and then how and where to invest pension and other monies for maximum growth.

I. Pension Plans

Definition: Pension plans are used for accumulating money during your working years to support you financially in your retirement, post-working years.

Pensions maximize money by avoiding taxes during their growth years. Taxes are only paid when you take distributions – usually at retirement (for most pension types, see below). Your employer might even add to your pension contributions, up to a certain percentage, called employer "matching." Ask.

Funding pensions should be done only after fully paying your housing costs, except where your employer matches pension contributions. This is free money you don't want to miss.

Pension plans are important if you want more money, because they make and save you money in these important ways:

- Investments grow quickly because they grow free from taxes.
- Your employer's matching pension contribution equals free money (possibly even better than free ice cream).
- Pension plans save you money because you pay less tax. Certain pension contributions are deductible from income.

Pension Plans – Basic Mechanics

Sponsorship (management) of pension plans:

- 401(k) – Company as sponsor, regular and defined benefit pension plans. Company sets this up for you.
- IRA (individual retirement account) – You as sponsor, traditional and Roth pension plans. Your bank can help you set this up – it's a very common service.

Who contributes and maximum amounts allowed:

- 401(k) – You, as employee, up to $18,000 annually (currently). The company might match your pension contributions.
- IRA – You, as individual, up to $5,500 annually (currently).

Federal income tax: All pension monies grow tax free.

- 401(k) – Contributions are deductible. Distributions are taxed at time taken out – at your then income tax rate.
- IRA (traditional) – Contributions are deductible. Distributions are taxed at time taken out – at your then income tax rate.
- IRA (Roth) – Contributions are not deductible. Distributions are not taxed because the money you contributed was already taxed as income when you earned it.

Additional Pension Information

- Payouts can be a set amount: 401(k) "defined benefit" plan.
- You can have a 401(k) and an IRA at the same time.
- A SEP plan is for self-employed persons.
- There are pension rules regarding loans, early withdrawals, etc.

Pension information: www.FinancialBananaSplit.com

Retirement and Pension Quotes

- "There's one thing I always wanted to do before I quit . . . retire!" (Groucho Marx, comedian)
- "I'm retired. Goodbye tension, hello pension!" (Anonymous)

II. a) Investing: Securities

Every once in a while, there's a story in the news about a group of people, usually co-workers, who win and split a multi-million dollar lottery ticket. They pooled their cash (resources) and bought lottery tickets as a group.

It's the same basic idea when you purchase a share of company stock: a group of people pooling their resources so each individual has a piece of ownership in a larger enterprise. The same is true when you buy a company's bond: You and other individuals have each purchased a small part of the company's larger bond issue.

Bonds can also be issued by governments. Bonds issued by the federal government are treasury bonds or notes. Bonds issued by a state, county, or city are municipal bonds.

Both stocks and bonds are known as securities. Why are they called securities? Because you have secured ownership in either the company's assets (stock) or its obligation to repay its debt (bond) to you.

A type of security that owns the stocks or bonds of many different companies is known as a mutual fund. They might be sold as a traditional mutual fund, an ETF, or an index fund. Their differences are explained later in this section.

Stocks pay periodic cash known as dividends based on the company's earnings. Stock value is mostly affected by a company's earnings: When earnings rise, the stock value usually goes up, and when earnings decline, the stock value usually goes down.

Bonds pay periodic cash known as interest based on the interest rate at the time the bond was issued. Bond value is mostly affected by federally set interest rates.

When interest rates rise, existing bonds decline in value. When interest rates fall, existing bonds rise in value. Why? Because if newer bonds have a higher interest rate than older bonds, you're willing to pay more for them (premium). And if newer bonds have a lower interest rate than older bonds, you'd want to pay less for them (discount). Learn more at www.FinancialBananaSplit.com.

II b) Investing: Principles

I offer the following "classic" investing principals not to make you an expert, but to give you familiarity with investing enough that you'll be able to do research and use the information presented throughout this book to make thoughtful investment choices, ones that power you towards the American Dream.

Speculating versus Investing

Want to achieve the American Dream? Then stick to investing your money, not speculating. Why?

A short-term investment (less than one year) is called speculating, and it is basically gambling. Why? In the short term, the markets don't necessarily reflect realistic values – prices are more emotionally driven. If you need to sell, you're risking selling at a loss.

A long-term investment (10 years or more) is called investing because it rides the wave of market fluctuations and generally returns to a realistic valuation. Use this for retirement savings.

Anything can happen at any time, and a longer term tends to smooth things out. The typical economic cycle usually lasts about 12 years from Good > Bad > Good. Investing uses the long term as leverage to grow. Speculating does not – it gambles on a quick profit.

Want to practice speculating or investing without using real money? Find real-time market play at www.FinancialBananaSplit.com.

How's the Weather?

Want to achieve the American Dream? Then make a little effort to understand what you're buying before you buy it.

If you were considering relocating, you'd gather basic information about the new area before deciding to move there, such as:

- Year-round weather
- Housing costs
- Cost-of-living average
- Employment opportunities
- Proximity to recreation
- School information, etc.

Before buying securities, you should also gather basic information.

Stocks and Funds

- Current and historical price per share
- Current and historical EPS for the company (see later)
- Current and historical general stock market levels and how this stock's price tracked these markets
- Dividend history
- Quality rating

Bonds and Funds

- Effective interest rate you'll receive relative to "stated" interest rate (see later)
- Current 10-year treasury bond (note) price and yield
- Historical trends for both of the above
- Quality rating

Plan and Goal

Want to achieve the American Dream? Then you need a plan and a goal. A plan is for taking steps. A goal is what you measure your steps against (progress). A plan can be simple. The most important part is sticking to it.

Your plan needs to be flexible to account for unforeseeable changes while still continuing towards your goal. Example: Goal – Save $1,800 in one year. Plan – Set up an automatic transfer with my bank for $150 per month from my checking to my savings account. Add extra money when available if one month a financial emergency prevents me from contributing.

Risk versus Return

Want to achieve the American Dream? Then how much risk or loss are you willing to take for a higher return? This is the basic question of risk versus return. You only take more risk because you expect a greater or better outcome than from a less risky investment. It's foolish to put your money at high risk. Save gambling for Las Vegas, where your odds are probably better and casinos bring you free drinks. Gamble only with what you can afford to lose, not with your housing, savings, or retirement money.

The higher your risk, the higher your return should be.

Double the current 10-year treasury yield is generally where risky investment territory begins. See www.FinancialBananaSplit.com.

Price-to-Earnings Ratio (P/E Ratio)

Want to achieve the American Dream? Then understand if your stock is expensive or cheap to buy. Premium is expensive (bad). Discount is cheap (good). A stock's P/E ratio indicates how cheap or expensive it is today relative to its average price historically. Most companies' stock returns to a P/E ratio of 16, which is neutral. They follow the S&P 500 historical trend, which cycles about every 12 years. Each company has its own reasons for its current P/E ratio. A stock's P/E ratio equals its price per share divided by the company's earnings per share. This information can be found at the company's website.

Example: Stock price $60. EPS $5. 60/5 = 12 P/E. Stock is at discount. Stock Price $60. EPS $3. 60/3 = 20 P/E. Stock is at premium.

Multiple Income Streams

Want to achieve the American Dream? Then understand and develop multiple income streams. This refers to income from multiple sources, which can include job salary, income from rental properties, investment income, hobby income, part-time job income, your own business, etc. Use the extra income to fund additional sources of cash flow. The goal is early retirement with multiple income streams.

Automatic Deductions

Want to achieve the American Dream? Then use this "set it and forget it" method to grow your money. Monies directed by you to be automatically deducted from a paycheck or bank account to be put into savings/pension/ investment accounts are automatic deductions. This supports the "out of sight, out of mind" concept and is a stepping stone on the path to the American Dream. If the contribution to your pension, house down payment, mortgage, investments, etc. is deducted from your paycheck before you ever see it, then you don't miss it. You'll automatically adjust your lifestyle and budget to fit.

Pay Yourself First

Want to achieve the American Dream? Then choose investments that reinvest income or pay you directly instead of receiving nothing. When purchasing securities, this refers to only buying securities that pay dividends or interest. You're investing and risking your money. Shouldn't you get paid for it? Some investors believe companies that pay dividends are more trustworthy because they always need to insure a good cash flow. This way, they can always pay shareholder dividends. This makes them potentially less risky investments. You receive dividends even if your securities have gone down in value. This helps steady emotions during market ups and downs (volatility).

True Story – Dividends

A few years ago, I bought several hundred thousand dollars of a mutual fund at $11 per share. It paid a 7.25% federal tax-free dividend income on my principal investment. Due to economic variables (none affected the ability of this fund to generate its dividend) its price fell 66% to five dollars per share. They paid their dividend like "clockwork" – on time and exactly to the penny – even though the fund lost two-thirds of its market value.

It was a rough ride emotionally, but I didn't sell and continued to collect my dividends.

Several months later, the fund reversed its downward trend and went up 50%, again due to market variables having nothing to do with the financial health of the fund itself. I was receiving income while owning the fund through a volatile period. It kept me from selling for a loss, which would have been a big mistake. Find this and other income funds at www.FinancialBananaSplit.com.

Dollar Cost Averaging

Want to achieve the American Dream? Then follow a steady, long-term investing schedule. This means buying the same dollar amount of the same security each period as set by you: monthly, quarterly, annually, on your birthday, your pet's birthday, etc. Sometimes it's expensive, and sometimes it's cheap . . . It all averages out over time. This has proven better than trying to time the market.

Example: You buy 10 shares of XYZ Corporation stock every year on your birthday. One year, a share can cost $92. Another year, it might cost $121. Do this for twenty years, and your average price might be $106. You didn't over or underpay: the average price you paid is called "Goldilocks" – it's just right.

Buy and Hold

Want to achieve the American Dream? Then choose quality, believe in it, and never let it go. (Gee, too bad we don't apply this strategy to choosing spouses.) This means buying and never selling high-quality securities, whether bought as individual stocks or as a fund – you would keep the fund if it were highly rated* overall.

*Highly rated with a long history of dividend or interest payments. Large, well-known companies such as IBM, McDonalds or General Electric (S&P 500 listed) all qualify. For securities ratings: www. FinancialBananaSplit.com

Buying and selling what you hope is the next "hot" stock involves higher risk by trying to time the market. This reduces long-term returns by incurring broker fees and other charges each time you buy or sell and losses if you guess wrong.

Diversification

Want to achieve the American Dream? Then lower your investment risk by diversifying. This means owning different types (classes) of asset: stocks, bonds, commodities, and real estate. Owning a home is your primary real estate investment, so you've covered for this. All investments go up and down unpredictably over time: When one is up, another is down.

Familiar with the carnival game where you hammer a mole? Diversification is the same concept: You never know which mole is going to pop up, but if you place the same bet on all of them at the same time, you always pick a winner. The balanced mutual fund is an example of diversification. These funds are also known as "all in one" investments because they hold a diversified group of assets: stocks, bonds, commodities, international securities, etc. (see page 125).

Target Funds

Want to achieve the American Dream? Then don't pick securities – let a target fund do it for you. With these funds, you pick your expected year of retirement, and the fund automatically adjusts its mix of stocks and bonds as you reach your retirement age. It has more stocks for growth in the early years and more bonds for income payout in your later, retirement years. On my list (See Investing: Strategies), VFIFX is a target mutual fund.

The Rule of 72

Want to achieve the American Dream? Then know how long it takes for your investment to double. This formula shows the number of years it takes an investment to double at an estimated growth rate or "yield" (through appreciation, dividends, interest, or a combination thereof) using reinvesting. You simply divide 72 by your expected annual yield.

Example: You invest $2,000, which pays an annual dividend of 8%. Then: 72 ÷ 8% = 9. It takes nine years for your money to double at an 8% yield with all dividends and interest reinvested.

Stock "Splits"

Want to achieve the American Dream? Then understand this basic mechanism of how stocks work. A stock "split" is when a company's stock price has reached a high price and the company splits its stock: It gives its shareholders two (or more) shares of half-valued stock for every one share they own. Split shares historically rise in value.

Compound Interest

Want to achieve the American Dream? Then understand and use this time-tested wealth creator. The most powerful factor in wealth creation is **TIME.** Nothing illustrates this better than compound interest.

Compounding means growth by reinvesting dividends and interest back into the securities that produced them.

This especially applies to pensions, where income isn't taxed. Your money grows fast because you're receiving income on this income as well as income on your original investment. Simple interest grows money slower. You only receive income on your original investment, not again on the income it generates.

Equation – Simple vs. Compound Interest

This equation shows compound interest rate growth to be triple that of simple interest rate growth: simple interest: 3 + 3 + 3 = 9 vs. compound interest: 3 x 3 x 3 = 27.

A compound vs. simple interest rate graph is illustrated below:

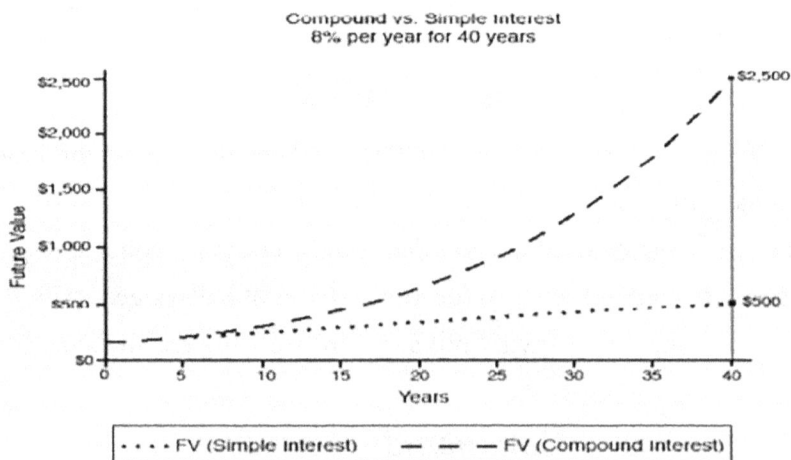

Compound vs. Simple Interest
8% per year for 40 years

As you can see, compound interest produced a result 500% greater ($500 vs $2,500) than simple interest.

Here's a pie chart with another way to view compound interest:

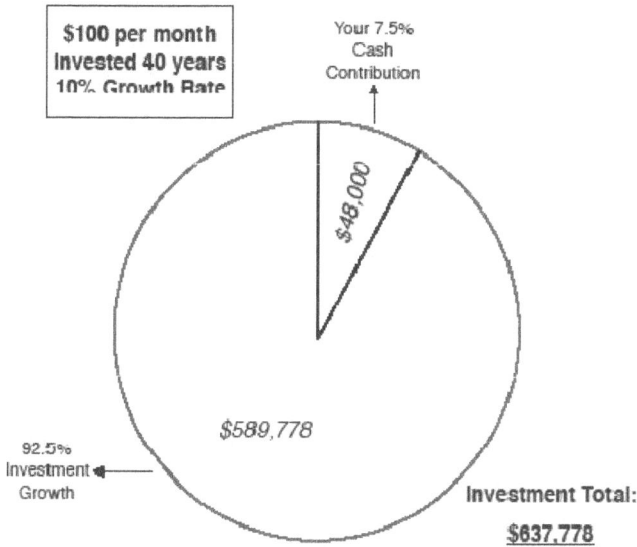

$100 per month
Invested 40 years
10% Growth Rate

Your 7.5%
Cash
Contribution

$48,000

$589,778

92.5%
Investment
Growth

Investment Total:
$637,778

This shows $100 a month ($3.34 a day) invested for forty years in an S&P 500 index fund. This fund has historically earned 10% per year with reinvested dividends, which is the basis of compounding. Your total contributions of $48,000 grows to $637,778.

You contributed 7.5%. Compound growth contributed 92.5%.

Think of it as: Easy + Simple = Millionaire.

True Story – June Cleaver and Compound Interest

A friend of mine from the Midwest (I call her June Cleaver, after the iconic mother character in a 1950s television show) was able to retire early, and both she and her husband (ex) were able to accumulate over a combined one million dollars.

How? They were middle-class working people who, through steady automatic deductions into their pension plans and leaving their monies untouched, let their investments grow through compound interest – earning interest on the interest their investments produced and then reinvesting it.

She used part of this money to buy a house – cheap – for her daughter during the housing meltdown of 2008 – another smart financial move. She did good, and now the market value of the house is almost triple what she paid for it. It's the "buy low, sell high" technique and mindset.

This story proves average income earners have a shot at financial independence. It just takes patience and following the basic strategies provided throughout this book.

An Easy-to-Learn Tasty Anagram

I = Interest
C = Compounding
E = Every day
C = Creates
R = Real
E = Easy
A = Additional
M = Money

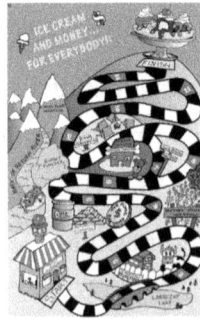

Illustration from the board game
Ice Cream and Money . . . for Everybody!!

THINK
I-C-E C-R-E-A-M
GROW RICH

Go to www.FinancialBananaSplit.com
to buy this board game.

II(c) Investment: Strategies

Mutual Funds, ETFs, and Index Funds

Want to achieve the American Dream? Then here's a way to buy securities that spreads out risk.

Funds buy and hold many securities. This is diversification. If one stock or bond fails, it's only a fraction of the fund's total value. Thus, it has little effect on the total value of the fund.

A traditional mutual fund is a professionally managed investment fund that pools money from many investors. It purchases securities to achieve a stated economic goal.

Exchange-traded funds (ETF's) are mutual funds too except they're "passively" managed – buying and holding securities – giving them lower operating costs and lower expenses for you. There are thousands of mutual funds and ETFs, each with their own objectives, investments, and level of risk, including high-tech, oil and gas, socially conscious, corporate bonds, etc.

Traditional mutual funds change price at the close of the business day. ETFs change price continuously throughout the business day.

Go to www.FinancialBananaSplit.com for a list of thousands of different mutual funds and ETFs.

The most general investments are "balanced" mutual funds. They invest in a moderate-risk mix of diversified securities.

These have proven to perform very well over long periods of time and are less risky than owning individual stocks or bonds.

A smart choice includes balanced funds with the lowest cost to own and the best long-term (10+ years) performance record. Four of the best are listed below. www.FinancialBananaSplit.com to view more balanced funds.

Many mutual funds have a minimum buy-in price of $2,500. The list below ranges from $500 to $1,000 dollars:

Symbol	Expense Ratio	Unit Price	10 Yr. Avg.	Morning Star Rating
ABALX	.59	$25.83	6.98%	*****
OAKBX	.79	$31.87	6.99%	*****
VGSTX	.32	$24.71	5.98%	****
VFIFX	.16	$32.04	5.88%	****

Index funds are a list of securities (stocks or bonds) that can be bought as a mutual fund or an ETF. Each index fund only buys from a specific financial index, which is a list of securities in a related financial sector: high-tech, pharmacy, oil and gas, banks, government bonds, etc. Their goal is to match the performance of their chosen financial sector. Examples: DJIA ("the Dow"), S&P 500, Nasdaq, etc.

The performance standard against which most investments are measured is the "S&P 500" (Standard & Poor's). It contains five hundred of the largest companies listed on the NYSE and NASDAQ stock market exchanges. It represents 75% of the US economy.

A Simple, Time-tested Investment Strategy

A basic investment strategy is to buy two low-fee, broad-based market ETF index funds: one for stocks and one for bonds.

Example: You buy one share of each type of Vanguard fund, a stock share of VOO @ $218 and a bond share of BND @ $80.

A classic money ratio is 2/3 (67%) stocks, 1/3 (33%) bonds. In the above example, buying an even number of stock and bond shares would give you 73% stocks, 27% bonds. Simple. This is within reasonable range of the classic stock/bond ratio. This strategy isn't perfect, but there's a thousand worse ones.

To do this, simply open a brokerage account (detailed below) with written instructions to buy per the example above. Fund it with automatic deductions from your paycheck or checking account – after paying all housing costs and pension contributions matched by your employer.

Review all investments at least every month to become comfortable with your brokerage statement and make sure you understand all charges and fees.

Easy: Opening Your Own Brokerage Account

Want to achieve the American Dream? Then it's time for you to open a brokerage account.

1. Open a brokerage account with your bank or online with a low-cost brokerage: Vanguard, Fidelity, TD Ameritrade, Scottrade, Schwab. All are good choices. Compare costs for fees, trading, balance requirements, etc. Www.FinancialBananaSplit. com for links to websites.

2. Specify that you want all interest and dividends generated from your investments to be reinvested. This is the basis of compounding, the way to supercharge investment growth.

3. Open a Roth IRA pension account where you opened your brokerage account. Transfer all brokerage securities into it. This allows faster growth because it grows free of taxes. Note: You can set up a Roth IRA as an individual even if you already have a company pension plan. You would contribute money into your company's pension plan before this Roth IRA, at least up to your employer's match.

4. Select a fund from the list of balanced funds, an S&P 500 index ETF fund, a mutual fund, or the broad stock market and bond index funds (Vanguard or similar low-cost funds) noted. Instruct your broker which investments to purchase and when.

5. Set up a monthly automatic deduction from your checking account or paycheck to go directly into this pension account, as much as you can budget.

6. Review your investment regularly to determine its relative performance before buying or selling. See www.FinancialBananaSplit.com for comparisons.

7. Increase your monthly contribution as you are able.

8. Enjoy a nice, early retirement. Buy me a drink when we meet at the cruise ship bar – thanks!

A new type of automated investment service is also available. It's low cost and uses sophisticated mathematics to invest your money in domestic and international stocks and bonds. It's based on your answers to their questionnaire.

Apps to assist with investing are also on brokerage websites. See www.FinancialBananaSplit.com for website links.

True Story – Pat

Let's revisit the successful investor equation:

Simple + Easy = Millionaire

Here's a real-life investment story from my tennis buddy, Pat. Pat went from complex to simple investing and bought this new sports car to celebrate his good decisions and fortune.

Pat is a smart, educated computer engineer in his 60s. He has a good income and lives a comfortable life.

He invested his money with a traditional full-service brokerage firm, paying them about 1.5% annually in fees plus other costs. Even though he'd had his money in the financial markets for decades, Pat never saw his financial picture significantly improve.

After losing much of his portfolio value in the 2001 financial crash, Pat decided to take what was left of his investments and transfer them into a low-cost S&P 500 index fund with Vanguard Brokerage Services.

I met Pat in 2014 at our local tennis group and immediately noticed his brand-new European sports car. I told him I admired his car, and he told me his investment story.

With his own investments under his own control, Pat doubled his money as he rode the rising tide of a recovering market. Pat's success is a real-life story of the investment equation:

Simple + Easy = Millionaire. It works!

Should You Hire an Investment Advisor? Pros and Cons

Want to achieve the American Dream? Here's two **secrets** for successful money management, whether you decide to use an investment advisor or not:

1. You must know the basics of financial investing.

2. You must develop a healthy relationship with money.

Why? Because you need to track and understand why your investments are performing the way they are whether you're working with an investment advisor or not.

Knowing this helps you see the bad times with an understanding of why it happened and calculating when it will turn around instead of "why, poor little me," panicking and selling at the low point (been there, done that).

Fortunately, these two secrets for successful money management are explored and explained in this book's Step One: Achieve Money Self-Awareness and Step Two: Gain Financial Literacy.

After you've read and understood this book's steps one and two, consider these additional points to help you decide if a financial advisor – and which type – is right for you:

- Don't hire a financial advisor to assist you if you only own "set it and forget it" S&P 500 and bond index funds. Just set it up and use a discount broker.

- Most discount brokers now offer low-cost "over the phone" services if you need to consult with a financial broker and "robot" broker services that take into account your risk tolerance and correct for market fluctuations using math algorithms.

- A full-service advisor's best use is really for investors who want full-time consultation on their actively traded accounts.

- If you don't want to handle most of your money for whatever reason, use a financial advisor. Consider putting at least part of your investments into simple S&P 500 stock and bond ETF funds in a 3:1 ratio with a discount broker. These funds should not be in your broker's "managed" account, because you're charged an additional fee for this.

- Track your broker's performance against the above funds over the long term and in consideration of major market fluctuations. This really helps you understand the markets. Your broker should help you with adjusting your financial mix to soften losses and take advantage of opportunities. Talk!

- What do I do? I use a Vanguard Brokerage services low-cost S&P 500 index fund as well as a financial advisor. However, the funds I have with my financial advisor are specialty municipal bond and energy funds – federally tax free. I don't pay him an additional fee for these. The funds pay him a 12B-1 fee, which is already built into their expenses. They can fluctuate wildly, but I understand the risks and like the steady income (cash flow rocks!).

III Retirement Planning

Retirement planning is the opposite of investing: Investing focuses on how much money you make, While retirement planning focuses on how much money you take.

The information learned in Ingredient Five: Investing can be applied to retirement planning because your investments still need to generate money – now more for income than growth. Once again, it's all about cash flow.

Calculating Your Retirement Budget

Complete your monthly budget on page 59. Use amounts relevant to your retirement years as follows:

Income – All items net of taxes: social security, pensions – including required distributions – estimated net income during retirement from part-time jobs, rental income, annuities, investments, etc.

Note: A "4% rule" is intended as the maximum amount you should withdraw per year in order to have your investments be a source of income until your death. More than this might require lowering expenses or increasing income.

Expenses – Your monthly expenses for housing will be much lower if you live in your home and have paid off its mortgage.

To better estimate general costs during retirement (food, utilities, etc.), account for inflation by adding 4% to your current budget expenses (for relevant items) each year between now and the year you'll turn 80. It's just a "guesstimate" based on average longevity.

Example: Current age = 35. Years until age 80 (death?) = 45. Therefore: 4% x 45years = 180%. Add 180% to each expense. A current $300 expense item + 180% equals $840.

Annuities

Annuities are life insurance company financial contracts. They're a combination of securities and life insurance with a minimum guaranteed income.

They're popular for retirement planning because the guaranteed monthly payouts might be more than you can comfortably withdraw from your investments over a long retirement period.

Annuities can be costly and complex, and you pay big commissions to brokers. They have high operating expenses and steep surrender charges (if you stop paying).

How do you buy the most cost-efficient annuities? Source: Directly from the issuing insurance company.

Type: SPIA (single premium immediate annuity). Why? You pay a one-time lump sum to the insurance company. This removes your risk of policy cancellation for non-payment. A fixed-payout annuity is more reliable than one with a variable payout. See what death benefit, if any, your contract pays. www.FinancialBananaSplit.com for annuity websites. Purchasing separate investments and life insurance is an option.

Kid Stuff

Investment information is also applicable to children. The Uniform Gift to Minors Act (UGMA) allows an adult to open a separate investment account for a minor and control it until the minor reaches majority age. It can be opened at most financial institutions – I opened a UGMA for my son. With investing, time is power and children have the longest investment timeline. Coverdale and 529 Savings Plans are other options. These programs are more structured/restricted to funding education.

Ingredient Five – Conclusion

Investing for Wealth and Retirement does not involve magic. The conditions to achieve your goals, occur around us every day. Understand and apply the information in this Ingredient to use these conditions to your maximum financial benefit.

7

Ingredient Six:
Goodwill and Charity

Goodwill and Charity are the cherry on top of the banana split. Its concentrated sweetness gives you purpose and helps direct resources so you feel good about your wealth.

Sir Isaac Newton, Money, and Universal Truth

"For every action, there is an equal and opposite reaction."
"Everything in the Universe is connected."
(Isaac Newton, 17th century)

Newton's Mathematical Principles of Natural Philosophy can be understood relative to our own actions: We generate energy and interact with all other energy in the universe. Newton proved that the amount of energy a body gives is equal to the amount of energy a body receives. This is known as a "universal truth." It applies at all times.

Example: "Where there's water, there's life." Astronomers look for evidence of water on planets because, if they find it, they know some form of life can exist.

Newton's concern was motion, not emotion, but everything in our universe has an energy component whether the source is purely physical, as in his famous gravity event – an apple falling from a tree – or thinking, which causes our brains to use electrical energy.

Example: Energy used for thinking can be transferred to and interact with external energy, as proven in a mind-only controlled drone race at a university. They used EEG (electroencephalogram) headsets powered by student brain waves (Cuthbertson 2016).

Money, goodwill, and charity also seem to be connected by universal energy. When you view and respect your money as energy, you pay attention to it and keep it under control, in order. The universe has order, and so should your money.

Putting money in order means accounting for and managing its inflow and outflow (energy = cashflow). This is consistent with the information in Ingredient One.

Review your work in Step One: Achieve Money Self-Awareness, to understand your current relationship to money and how it can evolve to be consistent, with a balanced energy flow.

What you do with your money, intentions and actions, all have an energy flow.

Contributing to worthy charities, people, and causes with good intentions (and not because you feel obligated or because it makes you feel better than someone else) generates positive energy. Somehow the universe "gets it," and the energy you receive back is equal and positive.

The result is often more money. How? I don't know, but in this world, money seems to follow money. The federal government "gets it" too: Charitable donations are deductible from income. This lowers your income tax liability.

True Story – Son's School

My son's school was seeking donations for new kitchen equipment. (In public schools, education budgets are limited.) One of the items needing replacement was a commercial dishwasher for $3,000. A grant paid for half.

My son is thriving. He has new friends and a B+ average – much higher than in his previous school, where he was in danger of failing. And he's graduating high school one year early. :) Since parental joy is priceless, I decided to help out financially. I donated $1500 for the dishwasher. OK, so that's that, and I felt good about my donation.

At the same time, I decided to renovate my first-floor bathroom. I had a plumbing estimate for $4,000. The estimate seemed high, so I sought other bids. I looked on the internet and made several calls to local plumbers, but none returned my calls. I thought I would have to go with the original estimate.

When I was dropping my son off at school, I noticed there was a plumbing contractor close by. I decided I had nothing to lose and might as well walk in and see if they were interested. Wow! For the exact same job, they estimated $1,850. I saved over $2,000, and the only reason I found them was because they were next to my son's school. I saved much more than my donation amount.

I don't know if it was coincidence, Sir Isaac Newton, the Universe, or God, but giving, goodwill, and charity seems to be the right way to live and in perfect alignment with this book's Whole Self Wealth Program.

Ingredient Six – Conclusion

Goodwill and Charity can be thought of as: "Whatever good things we build end up building us." (Jim Rohn). Understand and apply the information in this Ingredient to help you put good energy into our world for a beneficial "boomerang" return.

> *"Service to others is the rent you pay*
> *for your room here on earth."*
> —Muhammad Ali

8

Step Two - Conclusion

In Step One: Gain Money Self-Awareness, you learned how to check your emotions in order to deal with money in a reasoned manner consistent with your core values. The purpose of Step Two: Achieve Financial Literacy is to give you the knowledge and tools necessary to be productive and profitable in almost any financial situation. You should be able to evaluate most financial proposals or strategies through the filter of the information provided to determine your best course of action relative to your core values and overall financial goals. The takeaway is being able to act successfully on financial matters using the powerful combination of reason and knowledge.

COLLABORATE FOR WEALTH BUILDING

1

Overview

Definition

Collaboration is when two or more people join to combine property, resources, or obligations to do or create something.

Your money is more powerful when used to leverage the whole instead of being the whole.

"Two heads are better than one."

(Anonymous)

Specific to this book: Your money plus other people's money, when used collaboratively, enables you to become a homeowner and/ or target more money into retirement investments. By yourself, you remain a renter, live in your parents' basement, or retire later and less comfortably. In other words:

Goal: Rewrite your STORY and . . . unlock your DESTINY.

2

Whole Self Wealth – It's All Related

Collaborate for Wealth Building is part of the Whole Self Wealth Program because human beings are social creatures who thrive in an environment of shared values, skills, and resources. When all participants understand and employ all three steps of the Whole Self Wealth Program to complete a project, communication is enhanced. This leads to more agreement, fewer detours, and a more efficient path to everyone's American Dream.

Collaborate for Wealth Building relates to Step One: Gain Money Self-Awareness in that clearer understanding of yourself and your goals means more success in choosing appropriate people to collaborate with.

Collaborate for Wealth Building relates to Step Two: Achieve Financial Literacy in that successful collaboration on money matters is aided by understanding money: yours and your potential financial collaborator(s).

3

Collaboration - General

General collaboration is a smart, efficient way to live before, during, and after you're a homeowner. Collaborating saves time and money by saving you from having to do every part of every task yourself (Orsi,2009).

Example

You cook dinner Monday through Thursday for you and your family. If you collaborate with three other families and each family is only responsible for cooking dinner one of the four nights, the following benefits accrue to all:

1. Time Saved: Each family only has to shop and cook one of the four days instead of all four days.

2. Money Saved: You cook more portions when it's your day. This means more food bought cheaper in bulk.

3. Variety: Each family probably has several cuisine specialties, thus augmenting variety.

4. Quality of Life: Collaborative cooking naturally enhances community socialization, leading to potentially more collaboration, savings, and variety.

Collaboration – Explained

There are different parts and types of collaboration.

These enable you to successfully collaborate on assets and services, saving you money, augments cash flow, and also helps socialization, enhancing your quality of life, because collaboration means interacting with others. The goal is to efficiently and happily achieve the American Dream.

With this knowledge and skill set, you can:

- Save for a down payment on a collaborative house.
- Save for your own home while living collaboratively.
- Have the skill set and experience necessary to live financially secure when you own a home of your own because you'll have extra money to fund your financial investments.

Learning to successfully collaborate is an alternative to spending the rest of your life working without hope of retirement and wasting your money on stuff you don't need, with no way of breaking the cycle. Collaboration skills are a stepping stone out of this cycle on your way to achieving the American Dream.

Reasons for Collaborating

Want to achieve the American Dream?

Then use collaboration techniques to do the following:

- Enhance cash flow (saving money) and wealth building (house appreciation and cash to fund investments) to achieve the

American Dream sooner than later by having extra money to put to work.

- Everyone is giving something and getting something of equal or greater value than they would have if they'd done it alone.
- Collaboration allows you to connect and meet people who

share your goals. This is a social component of the Whole Self Wealth Program that moves you towards happy – as in rich and happy – while on your path to achieving the American Dream.

What Can Be Used for Collaboration

Anything two or more people place an agreed-upon value on, from objects to expertise, can be used for collaboration.

Examples:

- Objects: Anything of agreed-upon value.
- Spaces and places.
- Time: Yours and theirs.
- Skill or Expertise: The ability to do something correctly.
- Other people who possess any of the above.
- Past, present, future involving any of the above.

Collaboration also includes "bartering," where there's an equal-value exchange without money from at least one party. The possibilities and combinations are endless.

Ways to Collaborate

Definition: A collaborator is a part owner or user of an asset, defined simply as something of value.

- Collaborative ownership – Collaborators own a part interest in the same asset, similar to being a company stockholder. Example: Four people are each owners of the same house.

- Collaborative use or responsibility – Collaborators agree to collaborate on the same thing (owned or leased by at least one of the parties) or non-asset (childcare) service. Example: One person buys a lawnmower and agrees to collaborate with three neighbors. What does the owner of the asset receive from the non-owner users? What's a good trade? Childcare? Car repairs? Help building a fence? Massage therapy? Straight-out cash payments?

The answer can be whatever is agreed as fair value and moves everyone closer to the American Dream.

Aim for Success

More than good intentions are required for successful collaboration. Compatible goals, personalities, responsibility levels, resources, and values are also required.

Know and understand potential collaborators by assessing these qualities through background checks (explained later), especially if you're going to have legal liability or invest financially.

Collaboration ranges from simple to complex.

However, collaboration (like most things) can be reduced to the five basics of story writing we're taught as schoolchildren:

- **Who:** Direct/indirect? Long/short term? Changeable?

- **What:** Everything clearly identified? Understood?

- **Where:** Physical location(s) identified? Changeable?

- **When:** Definitive/flexible start, finish, duration? Changeable?

- **Why:** Clear on goal(s)? Reason(s)?

Conclusion: General Collaboration

An agreement to collaborate might only require a handshake, or it could involve or evolve into a more complex arrangement requiring some of the elements mentioned above.

The important point is for you to understand what you're getting into, learn from each collaborative experience, and access resources (legal/financial, etc.) as necessary.

For help, look for a similar group and ask what resources they use and how they use them. Contact your local chamber of commerce, the Small Business Administration (SBA) or your county clerk's office.

Www.FinancialBananaSplit.com for more information.

4

Collaboration For Home Ownership

Overview

Why collaborate with others on home ownership?

To own your own home sooner than if you didn't collaborate.

You benefit in several important ways:

- Better cash flow – paying less monthly to own than to rent.
- Your own home might be nicer than what you can rent.
- A wealth increase over time due to rising home prices.

This allows you to gain equity for a future down-payment.

The comparison on page 73 between ownership in a collaborative house and a one-bedroom rented apartment illustrates the dramatic cost difference between these two lifestyles. The one-bedroom apartment costs $1125 per month. A bedroom in your collaborative house costs $294 per month. Use the monthly savings of $831 towards the future down payment on a home of your own.

Collaborative ownership differs from owning a house by yourself because, when you have multiple house owners (shareholders), you're dependent on each other to buy and maintain the house both physically and financially.

This requires several documents unique to collaborative house ownership to insure all shareholders meet their financial, legal, and social obligations. These agreements are signed by all shareholders and become legal documents whose terms and conditions are enforceable in a court of law. See www.FinancialBananaSplit.com.

Keep originally signed documents in a bank safe deposit box with restricted access requiring at least two signatures.

I'll explain collaborative-related definitions and documents now so you can follow the financial pathway below and the financial/legal/social elements, detailed with examples, later.

Definitions and Documents

Key terms important to collaborative home ownership:

- **Shareholder** – Legal owner of a collaborative house.
- **Closing Costs** – Bank fees, title fees, prorated property taxes, etc. paid at "closing," when house ownership transfers. These costs add about 3% to the purchase price.
- **Term Life Insurance Policy** – An inexpensive life insurance policy taken on the life of each shareholder. The death benefit is payable to the house emergency fund to replace the lost house budget income and pay other related costs as necessary until a new shareholder joins the house. Any excess money can remain in the house emergency fund. Details should be stated in your house collaboration agreement.

154

- **The Deed** – It proves who legally owns the house. It's submitted to the bank to obtain a mortgage. There are different types of deeds for specific situations, explained later.

- **House Collaboration Agreement** – This document details what's needed beyond a collaborative deed and mortgage. It covers many aspects of collaborative home ownership living including space allocation, expense allocations, buying and selling shares of the house, and renting out your house share: max duration, who approves renter, how problems are resolved, right to sublet, penalties for non-compliance, payment of PITI, renter responsibilities, etc. These documents must be signed by all shareholders. All future shareholders must adopt and sign these documents.

- **House Budget** – This document details the estimated costs of maintaining the house on a monthly basis, including mortgage, property taxes, utilities, etc. It will be amended as amounts change. Each shareholder must pay their monthly financial obligations per this house budget or suffer consequences as specified within. House budget contributions are kept in a separate bank account with withdrawal restrictions, requiring two signatures. It's noted in the house collaboration agreement.

  Each shareholder's personal monthly budget, which should still be completed each month, should include separate amount(s) for house budget contributions.

- **Emergency Fund Agreement** – This document shows how much is contributed by each shareholder into the house emergency fund and how or when it's loaned and repaid. It's to pay a shareholder's costs if he or she is unable to make their monthly required house budget contribution due to lost or reduced wages. Penalties for late and non-repayment are given.

Each shareholder's original contribution into the house emergency fund is given from their personal emergency fund as saved prior to their becoming a shareholder. The house emergency fund is kept in a separate bank account. Restricted withdrawl authorization will require two signatures. It's noted in the house collaboration agreement.

- **Consent Agreements** (background checks) – These are separate agreements, one signed by each shareholder, giving the shareholder's personal identification information and permission for other shareholders to conduct a background check to review their financial and legal information. All shareholders have the right to review each other's background information to determine their suitability before making a final decison on collaborating.
- **Health Insurance** – Each shareholder is covered for medical expenses by their own personal health insurance policy. Health insurance links at www.FinancialBananaSplit.com.

Financial Pathway to Home Ownership

Here is a way to achieve home ownership by following the financial pathway of saver > shareholder > full owner. This can be done by saving as little as $8 a day.

The financial pathway can be modified to fit your particular financial circumstances, taking more or less time. It depends on your ability to save and the cost of the house, including real estate taxes, financing costs, down-payment amount, maintenance, utilities, renovations, etc.

Ways to save more by spending less using collaboration techniques are examined in Part I: Collaboration – General.

The financial pathway amounts include down payment plus emergency fund plus closing costs for the collaborative house first and then for your own house in the future.

You can purchase a house without an emergency fund, but this is risky. If you lose your income due to injury or unemployment, you could lose your house to foreclosure. This would be a huge financial setback, and you'd be unable to qualify for a mortgage, either for a collaborative house or your own, for seven years.

The advantage of contributing first as a shareholder is that your contribution need only be equal to your shareholder percentage, not the total amount needed to purchase the house by yourself.

Example: A $200,000 house to buy on your own would cost $36,000: $20,000 down payment + $10,000 emergency fund + $6,000 closing costs.

This same house to buy as a 25% shareholder costs $9,000: $5,000 down payment + $2,500 emergency fund + $1,500 closing costs.

Major reasons to start as soon as possible as a shareholder:

- Waiting to save $36,000 will take too long or not happen.
- You're missing out on thousands of dollars every year in free wealth by not receiving the benefit of rising real estate prices.
- The money you spend on rent pays your landlord's mortgage and property taxes, not yours.
- As housing prices rise, you'll need more money to buy the same house. You'll be caught in the cycle of never being able to catch up with the funds needed to purchase your own home.

Financial Pathway: A>B>C>D

Progression: Saving > Collaborate > Sell > Full Owner

(A) Saving On Your Own

Example: For a house price of $200,000 dollars, $9,000 is the total cash needed to become a 25% shareholder:

- Save $8 x 365 days (1 year) = $2920 dollars
- Save $2,920 x 3 years = $8,760 dollars

In this example, the amount of money saved in three years, $8,760, is almost equal to the amount needed to purchase your ¼ share, $9,000. If you know these numbers in advance, you'll likely save the additional $240 needed to join this collaborative house.

These numbers are realistic, but your actual numbers can vary based on the price of the house and number of shareholders splitting the costs, etc.

(B) Collaborate – Owning with Others

- $50,000 = Beginning shareholder value (1/4 of $200,000).
- $75,000 = Future shareholder value (five years?) (1/4 of $300,000). A result of house value appreciation.

(C) Selling Your House Share

- $37,500 = Cash in hand after selling your house share:
  You sell your share for $75,000. Use $40,000 to pay off your part of the house's mortgage. Thus: $75,000 - $40,000 = $35,000. (You reduced your share of the house's mortgage by $5,000 – from $45K to $40K – making monthly mortgage payments.) Plus $2,500 refund from the house Emergency Fund.

(D) Buying Your Own Home

- $37,500 available to use towards a home of your own.

Your income amount must qualify if you apply for a mortgage. There are several ways to accomplish this. See Financial Considerations – Ownership Percentages and Legal Considerations in the following section.

Congratulations! Having been a shareholder, you've learned a lot about the financial mechanics and other responsibilities of home ownership.

Considerations for Successful Collaborative Living

It's vital to make your best attempt to enter a venture of this magnitude with people who are compatible for the duration of your house collaboration (three to five years?).

The following social, legal, and financial considerations need to be discussed and agreed upon in writing by all shareholders.

Social – Your Livability Wish List

To give your collaborative house its best chance to succeed, review this list of livability concerns and determine which are your "needs" versus "wants" (explained in Step One: Gain Money Self-awareness).

Choose your house and potential shareholders accordingly:

- Bathroom: Do you want/need your own, or is sharing acceptable? Must you have your own bathtub, or is a shower okay if the house has a bathtub? Is the bathroom access direct or indirect from the bedroom?
- Parking: Is a garage a must, or is a driveway okay? Is there street parking for visitors? Boat or trailer parking available?
- Yard: Do you need space for a garden, pet, children?

- Storage: What are your needs? Special requirements? Basement or outside shed okay? Attic useable as storage?
- Kitchen: Is it big enough for your cooking/dining needs? Are the appliances okay? Do you need a dishwasher, storage, eat-in-kitchen seating? pantry? Is there good natural light?
- Extra Room: Do you need an office? Extra bedroom?
- Heating and Cooling: Are separate utilities available? How do you divide costs? (see House Operating Expenses).
- Quality of Life: Do you need a smoke-free house? Quiet house? Do you want to be able to have overnight guests and parties on the weekends or watch sports in the living room?

Testing your livability first in a collaborative house gives you a better understanding of your "must haves" for your own home.

Legal Considerations

There are unique legal issues when you buy a house as a shareholder, whether you're part of a group that's just starting or you're buying a house share from a shareholder in an already existing collaborative house.

Background Checks

You enter into legally binding contracts when you agree, in writing, to collaborate on ownership of a house: deed, mortgage, property taxes, etc.

It's important to know the complete financial and criminal history of each potential shareholder to lower the risk of default and maximize your chances for success in a collaboration. The basic way to obtain full disclosure for each shareholder is to have each sign a consent agreement, which gives all shareholders the right to conduct a complete background check on each other. You'll need to obtain a current copy of each person's driver's license, social security card, passport, bank statements, pay stub, and other relevant documentation.

Go to: www.FinancialBananaSplit.com for background check information and a sample consent agreement.

The Deed

Regulations vary from state to state as to what type of deed (the document recorded by the county clerk that determines property ownership) is acceptable.

You also need to know what type of deed your lender accepts. The deed determines rights, responsibilities, and how you can sell your share. For example: A suitable deed for unmarried persons buying a property together is a "TIC" (tenancy in common). This deed gives you each undivided ownership of the entire property. It doesn't specify ownership or responsibility for specific areas (for example, who gets which bedroom). A separate shareholders agreement is needed for that purpose. Most importantly, the shareholders agreement allows you to sell your house share independently of the other shareholder(s).

With a TIC deed, it's important to have this separate shareholders agreement stating who will live where in the house and the rights of each shareholder to sell their share. (See previous section on shareholders agreement.) Example: Other shareholders have the "right of first refusal" at what selling price? New shareholder(s) must agree and sign the current shareholders agreement, etc.

With a TIC deed, upon a shareholder's death, their share passes to their heir. In a joint tenancy deed, upon a shareholder's death, their share passes to the other shareholders.

A company (LLC, etc.) can also be formed to buy a house. This limits legal exposure to a shareholder's non-house assets.

As you can see, there are different legal and financial structures to consider before purchasing a house collaboratively. See www. FinancialBananaSplit.com for entity types.

Zoning Regulations

Your county, city, or HOA may have limits and/or requirements on your ability to use your house as you see fit:

- Parts of house that can be used for living (basement? attic?).
- Number of unrelated persons who can live in one house.
- Restrictions on the number of dwellings per lot.
- Limits on building sizes by square feet or height – important if you're buying vacant land or plan to add an addition or house to your present land.
- Additional requirements for multi-unit housing.
- Building codes concerning remodeling and outside structures.
- HOA (home owners association) restrictions on collaborative housing and renters.

Financial Considerations

The most important financial point to consider when buying a collaborative house as a shareholder is to verify all parties can afford this house now and later. Review your potential collaborative owners: background checks, income tax returns, pay stubs, etc.

Ownership Percentages

When you collaborate on a house, there are numerous ways to split ownership percentages based on the type of financial structure you use:

A. The mortgage can be one for the entire house or a "fractional" mortgage, where each shareholder is only responsible for their share of the collaborative house's mortgage (lender approval needed).

B. Examples where all shareholders all have equal ownership:
- All shareholders pay the same amount of principal, assume the same amount of mortgage debt, and receive equal space in the house.
- One shareholder(s) pays more of the down payment, but the other shareholder(s) pays more of the monthly mortgage cost, equalizing cash contributions over time. Make a schedule of payments, signed by all shareholders.
- Different contributions of down payments, mortgage payments, and labor and materials towards home improvements are valued as agreed-upon financial contributions as scheduled and signed by all shareholders.

C. Examples where shareholders have unequal ownership:
- Different financial contributions: Cash, monthly mortgage payments, labor, and materials are agreed to have different values due to timing, market, etc.
- Equal financial contributions: The house is divided in an agreed-upon way where one part is valued differently than another part, giving each shareholder a different valuation.

Example: One shareholder has a bedroom and full garage use, and the other shareholder has a bedroom but no garage use.

Mortgage Document Requirements

Legal: The deed as recorded by the county clerk's office. Financial: As shareholders, each person has to show proof to the bank issuing the mortgage of available down-payment monies and incomes sufficient to cover monthly housing costs of principal + interest + taxes + insurance (PITI).

Mortgage Duration

A 30-year fixed-rate mortgage is the best way to go because it's the most realistically affordable. Also, no surprises: Your monthly mortgage cost is always the same no matter how interest rates change in the economy. And you can repay it early, saving thousands in mortgage interest if there is no prepayment penalty in the mortgage document.

A shareholder will receive credit (a lowering of the amount he or she owes on their mortgage principal) equal to any additional mortgage principal contribution he or she makes. This should be included in the house collaboration agreement.

Risk Mitigation Measures

Everything will go great in your collaborative house until a shareholder loses their income for several months or dies.

Actions are important to take as an individual, as noted in Step Two: Gain Financial Literacy, as well as when collaborating on a house. These measures can help you avoid severe financial disruptions:

1. Buy term life insurance policies on the life of each shareholder. Name the house emergency fund as the beneficiary in all shareholder's policies paid by the house emergency fund.

2. Each shareholder needs to be covered by health insurance so they don't have to make the choice between paying for medical care or their share of required house contributions.

3. Set up a house emergency fund to cover PITI (principal + interest + taxes + insurance) and other house expenses in case a shareholder has a job loss or lower income for a time. This is critical to the financial survival of a collaborative house.

The emergency fund should be equal to a minimum of six months of PITI to avoid financial problems and risk of foreclosure. Each shareholder should contribute an amount equal to their percentage of house ownership. Example: Emergency fund total = $10,000 dollars. If four shareholders each own 25% of the house, then each shareholder's contribution would be $2,500.

House Operating Expenses

The basic costs of operating a collaborative house (PITI + repairs + maintenance + utilities + internet + television, etc.) can be divided among its owners using any one of these formulas:

- Ownership percentage: This is the percentage of the house owned by each shareholder as stated in your deed or the percentage stated in your house sharing agreement as agreed upon and signed by all shareholders.

- Square foot percentage: This is the amount of space each shareholder owns as noted in your house sharing agreement as agreed upon and signed by all shareholders.

- Utilities: You can divide the house utility expenses by square footage owned or used, or by power usage if there's a way to determine who uses what in cases of extreme differences. Write this as an addendum to your house sharing agreement and have all shareholders sign it.

As it's impossible for me to know everyone's circumstances, use these scenarios as a guide to help develop your own way(s) to equitably divide your collaborative housing costs.

The only "must have" is a written agreement, signed by all shareholders, understanding and agreeing to the division of ownership and terms for buying and selling house shares.

Conclusion:
Collaboration for Home Ownership

There are many things to consider when collaborating with others, especially with house ownership. The other shareholders become your business partners.

Keep this dynamic in mind when going through rough patches, keeping your goal of owning your own home always present.

To give yourself the best chance of success, do your homework and be flexible while living with others. Remember: It's the tree that bends in the wind that withstands the storm, not the immovable oak.

To view case studies involving collaborative housing, go to www. FinancialBananaSplit.com.

5

Step Three - Conclusion

In Step One: Gain Money Self Awareness, you learned how to understand and develop a positive relationship with money. In Step Two: Achieve Financial Literacy, you learned the mechanics of how money works and how to make it work for you. In Step Three: Collaborate for Wealth Building, you learned how to increase your wealth working with others while incorporating the knowledge gained in Steps One and Two.

Story Time

Your Financial Future: Serious or Delirious?

This story provides a time-line view of what can happen in your financial life if you follow (or not) the information provided in Steps One, Two and Three.

Once upon a time, there lived two young women who were close friends, yet each differed greatly in their financial outlook: Dottie Do-whatever spent her money (and then some) as soon as she got her paycheck, living in the moment, not a serious thought about her future. Samantha Strong-saver thought about her future: living in her own home, having nice things, and traveling to exotic vacation destinations.

Samantha Strong-saver

Age: 23

Education: Community college

Occupation: Asst. Mgr. - retail

Family: Youngest of two children. Father not present. Working mom.

Residence: Shares apt. with roommate

Owns car: Yes – older, no payments

Dottie Do-whatever

Age: 23

Education: High school

Occupation: Asst. beautician

Family: Oldest of three children. Father works. Mother is a homemaker.

Residence: Parent's home – basement

Owns car: Yes – newer with monthly payments

Samantha embraced the Whole Self Wealth Program in this book by following through on Step One: Gain Money Self- awareness, Step Two: Achieve Financial Literacy, and Step Three: Collaborate For Wealth Building. Dottie did not.

Their stories illustrate the results and consequences of respecting yourself and your money . . . or not.

Step One: Gain Money Self-Awareness

Goal: To understand your core Self and how money affects you emotionally, spiritually, intellectually, physically, financially in order to deal with money successfully. This promotes Whole Self Wealth.

Strategy: Read and use techniques in this book's Step One: Gain Money Self-awareness and play the board game *Ice Cream and Money . . . for Everybody!!* (www.FinancialBananaSplit.com)

Actions Taken

Samantha Strong-saver

I read Step One: Gain Money Self-Awareness in Building Your Best Financial Banana Split and bought the board game Ice Cream and Money . . . for Everybody!! to play while reinforcing my book knowledge. I completed the three-part exercise in Step One and wrote my Power Money Mantra to keep me focused on financial goals.

Dottie Do-whatever

I don't see a need to change anything. I'll just continue buying my lottery tickets and live the dream life when I win my millions. Until then, getting by is good enough. I'll just do "whatever."

Results

Samantha Strong-saver

Mindset changed from helpless to empowered.

Dottie Do-whatever

No action = No change.

Step Two: Achieve Financial Literacy

Goal: Study financial information and implement techniques to build financial wealth. This promotes Whole Self Wealth.

Strategy: Read and use techniques in this book's Step Two: Achieve Financial Literacy.

Actions Taken

Samantha Strong-saver

I'll develop a monthly budget to gain awareness of my cash flow situation. I'll evaluate for wasteful spending I can eliminate and start building savings with a monthly automatic deduction transfer from checking to savings. I'll open credit union checking and savings accounts and take their debit card to use for most purchases. I'll take their credit card because it has a low interest rate and fees. I'll use it only for emergency purchases. I'll use a 1040A income tax form to file my taxes because I have deductions for pension contributions and student loan interest. This reduces tax liability. I'll contribute the amount my employer will match to my pension plan and study the best funds to invest my pension monies in.

Dottie Do-whatever

I'll open a bank checking account and take the credit card the bank offers. It must be the right one for me, so I don't need to compare interest rates to other credit card offers. I'll charge anything I don't have the cash for, even if it's not a necessity. I'll pay the minimum balance due . . . when I remember. I'll file my taxes using the 1040EZ, because it's the fastest and easiest income tax form. When I go to church with my mother, I'll make a donation. I work for my money – it's for enjoying life now. I'll donate lots of money to charity when I win my lottery millions. For now, I'll just do "whatever."

Results

Samantha Strong-saver	Dottie Do-whatever
My FICO credit score is established and rising due to my low credit card use and on-time payments. My financial future is becoming secure due to the funding of my pension plan and my savings account with automatic deductions, assisted by using a budget. And I have better cash flow after receiving a larger income tax refund because I used the correct income tax return.	My FICO credit score is established and falling due to my high credit card use and several late payments. I forfeited the tax refund I would have received using the correct tax return because I just used the easiest one to file my taxes.

Step Three: Collaborate for Wealth Building

Goal: Gain financial leverage by sharing time/skills/resources to build financial wealth. This promotes Whole Self Wealth.

Strategy: Read and use strategies in this book's Step Three: Collaborate for Wealth Building.

Actions Taken

Samantha Strong-saver

I'll start a dinner-sharing program with my roommate and neighbors. This will save everyone time and money. I've saved enough money in the past three years to consider buying a house with others and stop paying rent. I'll do it! Turns out, my future husband, Steve, was one of the other collaborative house owners. A real cutie! After several years, Steve and I can sell our original house shares for a profit and buy our own home.

Dottie Do-whatever

I don't feel a need to change. I'm my own person – a unique individual. I don't have to share with others to have the life I deserve. Haven't won the lottery yet. My parents moved into a nursing home. Me and my siblings had a big fight over who gets our parent's house. Now we have to sell it. We spent thousands on legal fees. Guess I'll take my share of the remaining money and move into an apartment as someone's roommate. My FICO score is so bad no landlord will give me a lease to sign. I'll just do "whatever."

Results

Samantha Strong-saver

Moving steadily towards achieving the American Dream.

Dottie Do-whatever

Moving further away from the American Dream.

FICO & Net Worth Timeline Graphs

(The data in these graphs is further explained later in the book)

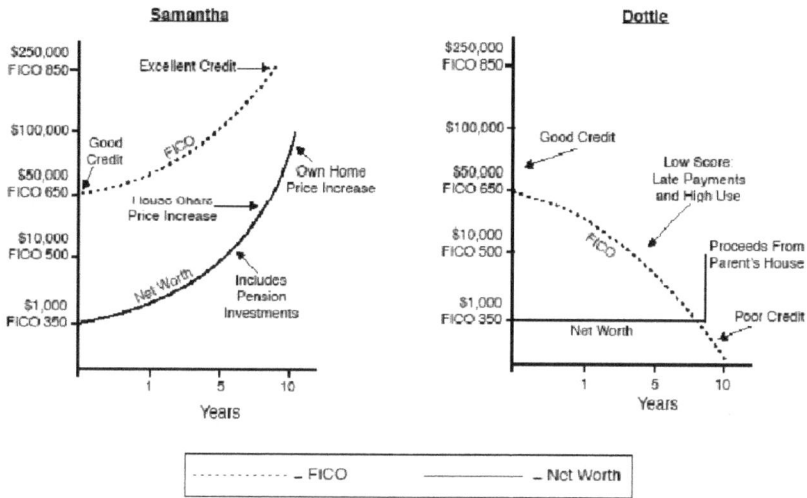

Samantha

$250,000
FICO 850—

$100,000—

$50,000
FICO 650—

$10,000
FICO 500—

$1,000
FICO 350—

Excellent Credit

Good Credit

FICO

House Share Price Increase

Own Home Price Increase

Net Worth

Includes Pension Investments

1   5   10

Years

Dottie

$250,000
FICO 850—

$100,000—

$50,000
FICO 650—

$10,000
FICO 500—

$1,000
FICO 350—

Good Credit

Low Score: Late Payments and High Use

FICO

Proceeds From Parent's House

Net Worth

Poor Credit

1   5   10

Years

················ _ FICO   ———————— _ Net Worth

STEP FOUR

A PATH TO
SOCIAL JUSTICE

1

Knowledge In Action

You've studied personal wealth creation in the previous three steps. Now let's use this knowledge to increase your economic and political power exponentially with other like-minded people.

I've been both a registered Democrat and Republican. Politics change. Parties change. Money is the constant. And money propels change.

Your grassroots monetary action (translation: your money) in concert with others can affect corporate behavior, policies and actions which in turn can affect political behavior, policies and actions. How? By buying stock with voting rights (generally the "common" stock of a corporation) in the company(s) you most want to influence or control.

Do this with enough people who hold similar values using an entity as your vehicle for stock accumulation and centralization (see below), and your group could have legitimate majority stockholder control of your chosen corporation.

It's called "corporate activism," and it's done all the time in the financial world. The motive is usually profit, but it can be used for any goal your group chooses.

Example: Your group has majority control of an oil pipeline corporation. A newly proposed oil pipeline route has raised strong objections from native Americans who've informed your engineers that this particular route would violate ancient, sacred tribal lands.

When brought to the attention of the board of directors of your pipeline company, a vote to authorize this route (which does not violate any federal or state laws) or to find an alternative route is now directly in your hands since, through majority stock ownership, you control the board of directors.

Political policy action? If the same choice is available to an oil pipeline company you don't have stock ownership in but your group does have majority control of the biggest employer in the county where this occurs, you could advocate through political channels for regulatory change, which could make this particular pipeline route less desirable than previously thought.

To occupy is a great idea. But where and what to occupy?

You can be much more effective changing corporate behavior by occupying seats inside a corporate boardroom as its directors than on the street it overlooks as detached protesters . . . three-piece suits and cigars optional.

Starting or joining a bank as a member (think: credit union) is another option. You can benefit directly from our country's central bank system - the Federal Reserve - that we as citizens support by paying taxes. It's **our** money! Example: The Federal Reserve lends banks money at a discount. The banks then lend this money, in the form of loans, mortgages and credit cards to the general public. The banks control how and who they'll lend this money to. If you own a bank as a credit union member **you decide** bank policy: who you'll lend money to and at what rate. Get it?

Other cooperative enterprises are also a path to power.

See: www.FinancialBananaSplit.com for related websites.

My purpose in writing this fourth step is not to take sides in a political debate. It's to illustrate that working within our current economic and political systems is a path that leads to real, lasting change.

Vote as a citizen and as a corporate shareholder. Both are necessary and important practices.

I hope to increase your economic power and voter influence by helping you see how, once again, small amounts of money can create big change in the same way that $3.34 a day grows into $637,778 and $8 dollars a day can buy ownership in a house. It all comes back to money and yourself.

Social injustice thrives on apathy. In the 2016 US presidential elections, 49% of us failed to vote. This sends a clear message to policy makers: corporations put up and ... people shut-up.

I believe Americans will increase their levels of voter participation, campaign funding, and political and economic influence by owning large blocks of voting stock in the very corporations whose actions they seek to influence – and owning or partnering with banks to better control their economic destinies.

It's the "beat 'em at their own game" strategy. The end game is not "You lose, I win."

The end game is "Everybody wins."

Why?

Because more citizens making more money directed towards a just and sustainable economy builds the best America possible.

2

Systems, Structures and Strategies – Briefly

Peanut Butter and Jelly

I feel it's important to understand the current United States political and economic systems in their historical context before studying business features and options. This will enable a clearer understanding of the purpose and benefits of the corporate structure and enhance objectivity.

Peanut butter and jelly are a great combination because they go together perfectly – they complement each other.

The same can be said of art and music throughout history: bebop jazz music and abstract art in the 1940s; acid rock music and psychedelic art in the 1960s.

And the same is true for political and economic systems: kingdoms and mercantilism from the 1500s to the late 1700s; democracy and capitalism from the late 1700s to the present.

The mercantile economic system complemented the kingdom political system because it advocated the hoarding of gold. It measured the economic wealth of a nation by its gold reserves. It believed new wealth could not be created – wealth was finite. And who had all the gold and wealth in a kingdom? The king. The results: mass poverty with no way out, colonization of foreign lands for raw materials, and constant warfare among nations for physical resources. The American colonies were the property of the English King for these reasons. 1776 was a huge year for new economic and political thinking.

The economist Adam Smith published *The Wealth of Nations*. He advocated for a free-market economy, where the wealth of a nation is measured by the total economic output of its people. And the economy worked best when it benefited all of society. He believed new wealth and full employment could be created by all people putting their capital to work (capitalism). Corporations were formed to help people pool their resources and participate in this new free-market (capitalist) economy.

Thus, a corporation is basically a vehicle for society-wide economic participation. It's not all just for the king. Proof? You can eat at McDonald's and also buy their stock.

Meaning: You're contributing to the profits of this multinational corporation and benefiting from your contribution ... at the same time!

And then Goldilocks ate the porridge that was . . . just right.

Oh wait. Great story but not the political one we need here.

The political story of 1776? The American colonies declared their independence as a nation free from the rule of King George III of England and became the United States of America.

So, how did that work out, this democracy and capitalism?

Oh yeah. The United States of America became the strongest and wealthiest nation the earth has ever seen.

Now it's time for you to understand and work within the system to get your fair share of the American Dream and, on your way, steer America to be the best she can be.

The Basic Corporation
Advantages

Whether your organization is planning to operate as a for-profit or non-profit enterprise, a commercial bank, or a credit union, there are many inherent advantages all businesses organized as separate legal entities share. These are as follows:

1. CONTINUATION – A corporation is a legal entity with its own life, separate from any natural person. It continues and doesn't end until it's formally dissolved. This gives a corporation the advantage of being able to continue operations indefinitely. You can prosper from a sale or pass it on for generations.

2. LIMITED LIABILITY – Debts and legal actions against the corporation are limited to collecting from corporate assets. This gives you the advantage of shielding your personal assets, such as your house and bank accounts, from creditors and lawsuits unless you've committed a crime: fraud, etc.

3. CAPITAL CONTRIBUTIONS – You can issue your corporation's stock to almost anyone, anywhere. This gives the corporation the advantage of being able to raise an almost unlimited amount of capital for operations. It's simply the price buyers are willing to pay for your stock issue(s).

4. LEGAL PERSONAGE – A corporation is a legal entity that can buy, sell, and own property and enter into legal contracts and assume debt. This gives the corporation the advantage of having financial power far beyond your personal finances.

Types of Structures
David and Goliath

The two most common types of corporate structures are the limited liability company (LLC) and the C corp.

The first type is simple and good for small companies. I call it the "David" of company structures. The second type is complex and good for giant companies. I call it the "Goliath" of company structures.

David: This is the limited liability company (LLC). It's a fast and simple way to form a legal business entity. It's technically not a corporation, but it has all four of the characteristic advantages of a corporation noted above. An LLC can be started by just one person or have many members. It cannot, however, issue stock, and investors must also be members. Profits are passed through directly to its members. This avoids double taxation of the LLC and its members. Most states have forms already developed for LLCs. You simply print them from your state's website, fill them out with the correct information, sign, mail, and pay a fee. Upon receipt, your state will register your new LLC.

As with any business entity, there is an annual report filed with the state and income filing requirements for the IRS.

Goliath: This is the C corporation (C corp.). Its complex documentation, filing, and regulatory oversight are generally done if your company has grown substantially and you want to issue stock to the general public. The C corp. (C relates to its section in the IRS code) is the structure we generally use when talking about corporations. Examples include Ford, Amazon, General Electric, etc. Profits are taxed at the corporate level at the federal corporate tax rate. They're not passed through to shareholders. However, shareholders pay taxes on any dividends received. The C corp. has the advantage of deducting many expenses including those for employee medical plans. It has all four characteristic advantages noted above.

The subchapter S corporation (S corp.): This is a hybrid corporate structure that shares some of the features of both the LLC and the C corp. The main reason the S is chosen over the C is to avoid double taxation on its profits – they are passed through to its stockholders and not taxed at the corporate level.

There are many other details and factors to consider when deciding to form a legal entity to conduct business.

See www.FinancialBananaSplit.com for more information.

Honest Operations

Whatever the entity's business, it **must** contain the following elements in its bylaws for operational integrity:

a) Financial Transparency – People get funny around money – especially when the money isn't theirs. Your entity *must* have a detailed, annual published audit performed by a licensed, unrelated, external auditing firm. I suggest quarterly audits as well. All the money must be accounted for in detail and explained in plain English.

b) Operational Parameters – What the business entity can and cannot do is vitally important to avoid misunderstandings and costly legal action. Are loans to members/stockholders/officers allowed? Limits? What and when is the entity allowed to buy or borrow, and when is it allowed to enter into contracts? Who has this authority? Majority vote needed?

Many of these concerns are addressed in standard legal documents used when an entity initially files with the state.

Banks

I discuss banks because, as credit unions, they can be established by, for, and of the local community.

They offer many financial advantages, including:

1. Deposits are insured by the FCUA up to $250,000.
2. They are tax-exempt non-profit organizations:
   a) This allows them to give lower interest rates on mortgages, car loans, and credit cards.
   b) The profits can be used to fund businesses that benefit the community such as food co-ops, etc.
   c) Profits can be used to pay higher interest rates on members' checking and savings accounts and CDs.
3) An S corp. is usually formed to charter and operate a credit union – a corporate structure discussed above.
4) Every depositor is a member, and every member has a vote in deciding bank policy and electing its board of directors. It's a true functioning democracy.
5) There is a national ATM credit union network.
6) Investment and technical assistance is available for credit unions in low-income areas through the National Federation of Community Development Credit Unions.

Most credit unions are state chartered (licensed) by the secretary of state or the state's banking division.

And the fun part? You get to name your credit union almost anything the members agree upon.

Bottom line: Money is power. Here's a path open to all.

Stock-buying Organizations

A stock-buying club can be set up as an LLC. Then it's a for-profit entity with no contribution restrictions. The problem a non-profit charity has is that it must continually seek donations because they are spent yearly. Charities are not set up to generate their own money. A for-profit entity is exactly the opposite: its financial goal is to perpetually self-fund from its own operations. Member investments are not depleted every year – they're constantly increasing in value. This prompts members to continue investing, and the cycle continues.

By investing in the voting stock of corporations, your entity gets a quadruple financial gain: 1) Members receive dividend income. 2) This allows them to buy more stock. 3) This generates more dividend income to purchase even more stock. 4) The stock value appreciates over time.

It's classic compounding. See Ingredient Five: Investing.

If your entity's goal is to influence corporate policy, this is a well-used strategy. Owning enough corporate stock enables you to replace the company president and board of directors with persons more aligned with your values.

You can also ally yourself with other likeminded shareholders. Your entity and these others could own a controlling interest in the corporation to effectively institute change. This happens all the time in the business world (see page 179).

Ten million members investing two dollars per week equals one billion dollars of stock purchased every year. That's a lot of power. It's basically the "change from within" concept: using the stock of a corporation to influence that corporation.

Also, dividend income and the sale of appreciated stock can be turned into a powerful cash weapon when needed to support your choice of policies and politicians. It can also be used to fund alternative companies and co-ops.

Geographic Strategy

Geographic strategy involves two levels: state and national. The state entities are better suited to work at the grassroots, local level, as their better acquainted with this level of political representation. National entities work more effectively at the national political level.

State-chartered credit unions belonging to a national association are an excellent example of this local / national dynamic.

A national association can be formed to coordinate multiple state entities and act as a clearing house for information.

3

Step Four – Conclusion

I've illustrated effective, practical plans to rebalance wealth and social justice in our great country.

They're action plans that can be implemented at local and national levels. They're for those who want to continue their good work and have their efforts net permanent results.

I believe it's always a good time to take positive action to work within our present political and economic systems to effect outcomes benefitting the majority of Americans.

If the counterculture of the 1960s had implemented these practices, it might have been a much more influential force in our world today, and we might be living in very different times indeed. (Would we all be required to wear bell-bottoms?)

"Democracy is the worst form of government, except for all those other forms that have been tried."

—(Sir Winston Churchill, English Statesman, 20th C.).

Got to www.FinancialBananaSplit.com for information and links to sites to help establish and operate various legal entities.

Book Conclusion

The purpose of this book is to show how the Whole Self Wealth Program helps you to Gain Money Self-Awareness, Achieve Financial Literacy, and Collaborate for Wealth Building, enabling you to achieve the American Dream: home ownership and financial security with emotional contentment.

By following this program, you will continually improve emotionally, intellectually, physically, spiritually, and financially, gaining a new understanding of your Self and using this knowledge to achieve the financial life you so richly deserve.

Add Step Four – A Path to Social Justice, to your knowledge and actions to take your quest for social justice (or world domination) to the national level.

Do your best, learn from your mistakes (I have), and contact me to share your stories. Pictures and videos are a plus.

No profanity, nude photos, or graphic violence please. www. FinancialBananaSplit.com.

I'd especially love to hear what you've learned from this book and board game and any of the steps you've implemented.

The board game Ice Cream and Money . . . for Everybody!! complements and reinforces all the information in this book.

It's fast-paced and fun to play – designed by the author (me). Go to www.FinancialBananaSplit.com to view and purchase.

Also, corrections are always appreciated for future editions.

Author's Attempt
at Prose and Poetry

If you don't learn how to control money,
The people who do know how to control money
.... will learn how to control you

Peace and prosperity complement each other.
Trying to force peace doesn't work because the action of
force is the opposite of peace.
Instead, force prosperity upon yourselves.
Then you'll have the resources to build peace.

We are but travelers between birth and death.
To own your own home
Lets you catch - your - breath.
Ahhhhhhh . . .

The truth is simple.
Ice cream is simple.
Money explained as ice cream . . .
Is the simple truth.

Bruce. A. Rowland

Note To Educators and Lesson Planning Guide

Invite local professionals from various disciplines to speak. This will enhance and reinforce learning by bringing experiences from "real world" professionals into the classroom:

1. Real Estate Agent – Property evaluation and purchase.
2. Mortgage Broker – Mortgages: qualifying and types.
3. Banker – Bank services: opening and managing accounts.
4. Insurance Agent – Insurance purpose: types and function.
5. Financial Planner – Investing: basics and strategies.
6. Non-profit Representative – Charity: purpose and goals.
7. Social Worker/Psychologist – self-awareness and emotional control.
8. Communications/Media Professional – communication awareness and control.
9. Accountant (CPA) – Tax preparation, filing, and planning.
10. Author/Writing Coach – To enhance self-expression.

Note: A free Lesson Planning Guide covering the first three steps of this book is available for download: www.FinancialBananaSplit.com

Bibliography
And Further Reading

Bibliography

Bogar, Dawn. *The ABC's of Self.* Florida: ABC's of Self Inc. Publishing, 2013.

Berne, Eric, MD. *Games People Play: The Basic Handbook of Transactional Analysis.* New York: Ballantine Books, 1964.

Cuthbertson, Anthony. "Watch: World's First Mind-Controlled Drone Race. *Newsweek.* April 25, 2016.

Capacchione, Lucia, PhD. *Recovery of Your Inner Child.* New York: Simon & Schuster, 1991.

McKay, M., PhD, M. Davis, PhD, and P. Fanning. *Messages: The Communication Skills Book.* Oakland: New Harbinger Publications, 2009.

Orsi, J. and Doskow, E. *The Sharing Solution.* Berkeley: NOLO Publishing, 2009.

Orman, Suze. The 9 Steps to Financial Freedom. New York: Three Rivers Press, 1997.

Vanguard Brokerage Services, Valley Forge, PA 19482

Further Reading

www.FinancalBananaSplit.com

Acknowledgments

Many thanks to the people who directly or indirectly helped me on my journey of writing and completing this book:

- Professor Patrick Tierney, Palm Beach State College, FL, whose creative writing class ignited my passion for writing.
- The students in the above class who, although I was somewhere between their fathers' and grandfathers' ages, accepted me as their peer and showed me kindness and encouragement.
- Dawn Bogar, author of *The ABC'S of Self* (2013). She was a catalyst in my decision to write my own book. ("If she can do it, I can do it.")
- Rachel Weaver, author of *Point of Direction* (2014). Her critique classes improved my writing skills and book focus. She recommended my first editor and enabled me to meet my main critiquer.
- Editors Jennifer Phelps and Lind Stirling, who helped me improve

my book to the point where it's hopefully useful, readable, and able to find an audience.

- Dave Schneller, financial critic and retired banker, who took pity on me as a novice writer of finance. Without his constant interest, I might have given up.
- Taylor Hilberry for graphic illustrations and Scott Charles for charts.
- My son, Adam, for being a soundboard to my many fragmented ideas, helping sort out the necessary from the nonsense.

The Board Game

ICE CREAM AND MONEY
. . . FOR EVERYBODY!!

BUY IT – PLAY IT – LEARN IT – EARN IT !

www.FinancialBananaSplit.com

About The Author

Being raised and having had a successful business career in New York, the author, his son, Adam (who is college bound), their dog, "Spikey" (who isn't attending college), along with their 1972 Jaguar, reside outside Denver, Colorado.

Mr. Rowland will continue to explore options for best communicating all things related to Whole Self Wealth in various formats for all who can benefit from this program.

www.ingramcontent.com/pod-product-compliance
Lightning Source LLC
Chambersburg PA
CBHW070530200326
41519CB00013B/2997